LIGHT YEARS by Billy Aronson
"The first act of a full-length play in progress, it all works perfectly, and the stunning end leaves you wondering what could happen

—D.J.R. BRUCKNER, *The New York Times*

PROOF by Jeff Reich
"Hilariously, farcically bitter."

—BRUCE WEBER, *The New York Times*

ALIEN BOY by Will Scheffer
"Dynamic and thrilling . . . Scheffer writes as if he's the dark side of Paul Rudnik."

—BARBARA AND SCOTT SIEGEL, *Theatermania*

THE ROTHKO ROOM by Stuart Spencer
"Clever."

—D.J.R. BRUCKNER, *The New York Times*

Ensemble Studio Theatre Marathon

› THE ONE-ACT PLAYS

2000

 FABER AND FABER, INC.
An affiliate of **Farrar, Straus and Giroux**

ALSO AVAILABLE *Ensemble Studio Theatre Marathon '99*

FABER AND FABER, INC.
An affiliate of Farrar, Straus and Giroux
19 Union Square West, New York 10003

Designed by Gretchen Achilles

Ensemble Studio Theatre is a not-for-profit professional theater founded in 1968 by Curt Dempster. It is located at 549 West 52 Street, New York, NY 10019. Marathon 2000: Curt Dempster, Artistic Director; M. Edgar Rosenblum, Executive Director; Jamie Richards, Executive Producer; Eileen Myers, Literary Manager; Daniel Selznick, Chairman of the Board

Contents

Ensemble Studio Theatre Marathon
2000

Light Years

2000 › BILLY ARONSON

ORIGINAL PRODUCTION

DIRECTOR Jamie Richards
SET DESIGNER Warren Karp
COSTUME DESIGNER Amela Baksic
SOUND Beatrice Terry
PROPS Cynthia Franks
PRODUCTION STAGE MANAGER John Thornberry
STAGE MANAGER James Carringer

The cast was as follows:
COURTNEY Anne Marie Nest
DAPHNE Sarah Rose
DOUG Paul Bartholomew
MICHAEL Ian Reed Kesler
All four are college students.

CHARACTERS

COURTNEY

DAPHNE

DOUG

MICHAEL

All four are college students.

TIME

Beginning of freshman year, about 6 p.m.

NOTE

Light Years is the first act of a full-length play also called *Light Years*, which takes the characters through four years of college.

The living room of a freshman double. Doors lead to the bedroom and the hall. The furnishings consist of a desk, a chair, a closet, a couch, and a crate.

DAPHNE *and* COURTNEY

DAPHNE So if I wear these sunglasses—

COURTNEY Philosophy.

DAPHNE They'll see me as—

COURTNEY Lit major, comp lit, philosophy, psych.

DAPHNE But if I go with this pair—

COURTNEY Engineer.

DAPHNE Engineer.

COURTNEY Exactly.

DAPHNE So I have . . .

COURTNEY The choice.

DAPHNE Right.

COURTNEY Deep or diligent. *(DAPHNE thinks.)* Or you could go to the picnic open, like me. Open to sunshine. Open to the breeze. Open to law school.

DAPHNE Right.

COURTNEY Any choice has its pluses. I'm just saying that before you get pegged, you should decide.

DAPHNE Right.

COURTNEY Same goes for the photo.

DAPHNE The photo.

COURTNEY On your desk.

DAPHNE Oh yeah.

COURTNEY That photo says, to those dropping by on their way to the picnic, that you have someone, and that you're taken.

DAPHNE Right.

COURTNEY I have lots of someones. But I'm not taken.

DAPHNE Right.

COURTNEY I have friends who are taken, but want to appear untaken. That's their business.

DAPHNE Right.

COURTNEY I even have a friend who has no one, but wants to appear taken, for strategic purposes.

DAPHNE Right.

COURTNEY So anything goes. It's all up to you. *(DAPHNE nods.)* So? Do you want to appear taken? *(DAPHNE thinks.)* Let's work backwards. Do you have someone? *(DAPHNE thinks.)* Have you ever had someone?

DAPHNE This guy, we'd talk about everything, one time it was raining and there were all these sounds. the noises were us, saying and doing those things, that people say and do.

COURTNEY So you have had someone.

DAPHNE I can't remember.

COURTNEY But you do want to have someone.

DAPHNE Yes. Yes.

COURTNEY So you'll put away the photo.

DAPHNE Right.

COURTNEY And the cross.

DAPHNE The . . .

COURTNEY Around your neck.

DAPHNE This is a cross?

COURTNEY It looks like a cross.

DAPHNE Right.

COURTNEY I'm not saying bury it, I'm just saying be aware.

DAPHNE Aware.

COURTNEY Of the whole question.

DAPHNE Uh-huh . . .

COURTNEY Born again. Or the other extreme. Free spirit.

DAPHNE Right.

COURTNEY We're talking about your most fundamental values.

DAPHNE My most fundamental values.

COURTNEY Exactly.

DAPHNE Which are . . .

COURTNEY Pursuit of truth. Love of humanity. I don't know.

DAPHNE Right.

COURTNEY Before heading to the picnic you need to ask yourself: Is that symbol rooted in the exact message you want to send out?

DAPHNE Right.

COURTNEY So?

DAPHNE I'll come up with the answers as we shop for a plant.

COURTNEY Shop for a plant? Now? (DAPHNE *sits frozen.*) Are you telling me . . . you want to skip the freshman picnic? (DAPHNE *sits frozen.)* Daphne. Outside that window, in a matter of minutes, our generation will assemble. For this chance to win a prime spot in their ranks you've spent your last three summers serving burgers, committed your Fridays to filing periodicals, and taken out loans you'll be repaying till you're disabled or forty or dead. So seize the moment. Select the impression that will leap from your front and ricochet through the crowd till you're burned in their brains as a—

DAPHNE Philosophical lit major who's not religious and not taken.

COURTNEY Good. So then . . .

DAPHNE I can't put away the photo. Because I can't stand up. My legs, something funny. I can crawl, I'm crawling.

COURTNEY Listen to me, Daphne. You'll be fine, because you're blessed with something that will get you through no matter what the world throws at you: you're pure.

DAPHNE Pure what.

COURTNEY Inside you, is a basic goodness and honesty that's special.

DAPHNE You see this after knowing me for two hours?

COURTNEY I saw this after knowing you for two seconds. The things I'm encouraging you to consider are icing on the cake. That's all. We just want the right icing, for so very fine a cake.

DAPHNE *(Sitting up.)* This is all so easy for you.

COURTNEY You think I'm the type who just, everything's easy?

DAPHNE I didn't mean anything bad.

COURTNEY I know you didn't. It's only that some people have tended to label me. You know. As the type. Gliding along. Not really meaning things. But the thing is, growing up, my mother couldn't be with us so I, always had to be the one smiling, but it isn't easy always being the one smiling, people don't realize that, but I need you to know that when I say things to you I really mean those things from my heart.

DAPHNE I know that.

COURTNEY Anyway. Before I open the door to let in potential escorts, let's both take a second.

(They sit. A "special song" plays from above. Instantly both go into a trance.)

COURTNEY Somebody upstairs has good taste in songs.

(They listen.)

DAPHNE Sleeping late on a snow day.

COURTNEY Driving home from the prom.

(When the song fades, they emerge from their trances. COURTNEY opens the door—to find DOUG standing there. DOUG raises his voice at the end of many declarative sentences so they sound like questions.)

DOUG The sunshine splashing across the banners? The flowers all over the place?, and everywhere you look the greatest people? Strumming guitars? Dancing around? Hugging? Every few steps a different song? Everyone so giving, so open? Can I come in?, great room, so near the main entrance?, so near the bathroom?, great view? *(Calls out the window)* Hey Mom, go home? *(To them)* So we're classmates, first-entry-mates? So . . . do I hug you? Shake your hands? Kiss your hands? Let me move your crate. *(He moves the crate.)*

COURTNEY/DAPHNE Thank you./Thanks.

DOUG Let me center your couch. *(He moves the couch, grabs his back.)* The backache'll be no problem since I'm already taking aspirin for a pulled thigh. What terrific hair you have, and eyes. The atmosphere of giving and kindness here is contagious?

COURTNEY Iced tea?

DOUG Everybody's trying new things? Reaching out? Why iced tea.

COURTNEY You moved our couch.

DOUG I've never had iced tea. Why have I never had iced tea.

Because, maybe somewhere along the line I was prejudiced? Smelled a skunk out the window and thought: iced tea? So I wrote off iced tea and lived in fear? But now it's time to leave the past behind and have iced tea? *(Calls out the window)* I'm fine Mom. *(To them)* The other thing I love here is that no one talks about grades or scores?, they talk about ideas? I wonder if even though on the outside there are so many differences between us, deep down we aren't really all the same?

COURTNEY Sugar?

DOUG Sweetheart? Darling? And if even though the individual conforms to society it isn't really society that conforms to the individual in the end. Actually I'll take it plain, here goes? *(He drinks, grabs a napkin, spits.)* Better head upstairs for another aspirin? *(Starts out, stops.)* Any time you need your refrigerator moved just give a knock? *(Starts out, stops.)* Will you guys be going to the freshman picnic?

COURTNEY Surely.

DOUG Can I juh-juh-juh- . . . juh-juh-juh- . . . juh-juh-juh- *(Grabs his tongue.)* join you?

COURTNEY Please do. *(He goes.)* Nice.

DAPHNE Nice.

COURTNEY You find him nice?

DAPHNE You think he's nice, right?

COURTNEY He moved the crate. He moved the couch. There's no debating it: He's nice.

DAPHNE Moving the couch hurt his back.

COURTNEY But he acknowledged it up front.

DAPHNE Right.

COURTNEY He can talk about his pain.

DAPHNE Sensitive.

COURTNEY Exactly.

DAPHNE Like Mark and Dave.

COURTNEY Mark and . . .

DAPHNE Dave, from my school.

COURTNEY Did you like Mark and Dave?

DAPHNE I should have. They were so sensitive.

COURTNEY With someone this sensitive you could discuss your philosophy.

DAPHNE Right.

COURTNEY But if you have concerns about shifting to comp lit or psych, he could discuss your fears.

DAPHNE Right.

COURTNEY Or your feelings about your faith . . .

DAPHNE Do I have a faith?

COURTNEY With him you could find out.

DAPHNE Any issue.

COURTNEY But he doesn't just talk.

DAPHNE Right.

COURTNEY He identifies a problem, then takes action.

DAPHNE Aspirin.

COURTNEY Takes aspirin, takes action, exactly. Which takes courage.

DAPHNE Right.

COURTNEY You should go to the picnic together.

DAPHNE Just the two of us?

COURTNEY He loved your eyes.

DAPHNE Both of them.

COURTNEY I noticed.

DAPHNE Think he might be . . . musical?

COURTNEY Were Mark and Dave musical?

DAPHNE Dave played piano.

COURTNEY This guy might well play piano.

DAPHNE Jazz?

COURTNEY I can see him enjoying jazz. Tapping, swaying.

DAPHNE Can you see us together?

COURTNEY On the dance floor. Leaning together. Strolling to the punch bowl. A single cup, passed back and forth. He shouts in your ear. You shout in his ear. He grins, you gulp, you dance.

DAPHNE He enjoys dancing?

COURTNEY Surely.

DAPHNE *(Ecstatic)* At last. *(Suddenly furious)* God.

COURTNEY What.

DAPHNE Why did I let my parents buy me a ticket to fly home over midterm break when I could have had them fly out here.

COURTNEY To meet Aspirin?

DAPHNE For once I get a guy who shares Dad's love for jazz and I can't bring them together till Labor Day when we'd rather be celebrating the end of our first summer living off campus together with a weekend at the shore.

COURTNEY Fly home for the Fourth.

DAPHNE Aspirin'll be seeing his mom.

COURTNEY If he rearranged crates for you he'll rearrange his schedule for you.

DAPHNE *(Embracing* COURTNEY.*)* I'm finally taking off.

*(*MICHAEL *enters with course cards.)*

MICHAEL Eight credits from each of groups one and four excluding a writing course other than those in groups two and three unless granted permission by professor, advisor, counselor, or dean. I could fill these out in time for the deadline but I'd rather insert that crate in my nostril. All day I've been feeling so much like a cartoon character that I have to keep pulling my skin to see if it stretches. *(He pulls his lips.)* Human. Hooray. *(He sits.)* So what if this *is* your third-choice school, right? You've already survived fifth-choice parents on a ninth-choice planet. So where are you from? How was your summer? Are you taking blah 101 so you can major in blah, or are you really pre-blah? Will you sign up for blah and go out for the blah or audition for blah? Oh, if you went to blah well then you must know blah who I met back-packing through blah on blah.

COURTNEY Iced tea?

MICHAEL Why the fuck not. *(She hands him iced tea. He drinks it all. He looks at them, they look at him.)* You guys going to the fresh-man blah blah?

COURTNEY Surely.

MICHAEL If I finish my blah should I blah?

COURTNEY Please do.

(He goes.)

DAPHNE But how will I pull it off?

COURTNEY It being . . .

DAPHNE Dump Aspirin for Course Cards.

COURTNEY Are you sure that's the move you want to make, at this point in time?

DAPHNE Jazz with my parents? What was I thinking. That's what I came here to crawl out from under. Aspirin was about to drag me backwards. Till Course Cards snapped his lips and cracked my shell. Allowed me to stop pushing. To let down my smile and accept the quiet. I live to be quiet. I shine when I'm quiet. Did you hear how quiet I was?

COURTNEY You were quiet.

DAPHNE I don't want to crush Aspirin. But I can't let him drag me back to my days of Mark and Dave.

COURTNEY I'll go to the picnic with Aspirin, leaving you free to invite Course Cards.

DAPHNE Invite . . .

COURTNEY March up there, mention you're going, ask him along.

DAPHNE You really see us together?

COURTNEY Midnight, late autumn, two figures, out from the library, across the leaves in slow motion, a few syllables, a few nods, then silence, then a muffin, from his hand, to your lips, to his lips, to his room.

DAPHNE Raisin?

COURTNEY What else.

DAPHNE You don't think he'll mind my cats.

COURTNEY You have cats?

DAPHNE I hope to. Someday.

COURTNEY They'll curl up on his lap as he watches his cartoons.

DAPHNE *(Embracing* COURTNEY.*)* I'm finally moving on.

COURTNEY But before heading up, I'd change out of school colors.

DAPHNE School colors.

COURTNEY On your top.

DAPHNE These aren't school colors.

COURTNEY Close enough. *(*DAPHNE *gasps.)* For your tryst with Course Cards, you'll want to steer clear of school colors.

DAPHNE He caught me in school colors.

COURTNEY We'll erase the misimpression from his mind . . . as I dig deep into my trunk, and cloak you in black.

DAPHNE Black. *(Thinks.)* You saved my life.

*(*COURTNEY *goes into the bedroom.* DAPHNE *goes to the phone, makes a call.)*

DAPHNE Pick up. I'm here. It's great. I won't be home for break. Call me. I won't be home this summer, I'm free, I'm flying, I can see . . . everything, all your crap, what *was* that. Call me I'll explain. You won't get it, how could you. You're so old. I've gone a million miles, you're staying still. You'll never get it. You'll never reach me. Call me.

(DAPHNE hangs up, moves around. DOUG enters.)

DOUG Everybody's starting to mingle in these little clusters?, the chicken smells great?

DAPHNE I'm not going.

DOUG Thank you for having the courage to stand up, to something so obligatory, so unnecessary, so how was your summer?

DAPHNE I'll drop in on the picnic later.

DOUG You're right, let the others break the ice? Your roommate already went but who cares, you're the one with the eyes, beautiful eyes? Did you like high school?

DAPHNE Did I . . .

DOUG A haze? Mine too?

DAPHNE I need some time . . .

DOUG So do I, before we go?

DAPHNE Please let me finish my sentence.

DOUG We're finishing each other's sentences? What does that say?

DAPHNE Nothing.

DOUG You're right, but as nothing was being said, what really happened?

DAPHNE Time passed.

DOUG Time passed, you're right, so I guess we should go?

DAPHNE I have plans. But my roommate will go to the picnic with you when she's ready.

DOUG Just me and her? Her hair lights up a room. It would be wonderful if she would hurry because my roommate's coming down and he has this tendency to whine that the earth is his ninth-choice planet?

DAPHNE That's your roommate?

DOUG I like him and I think he's great but he's always breathing on people and tagging along?, I tried to slip out while he was

doing his course cards but when he heard my plans he said he'd
be right down?

(DAPHNE hurries into the bedroom.)

DAPHNE Course Cards'll be right down.

COURTNEY Here's your outfit.

(DOUG follows DAPHNE into the bedroom.)

DAPHNE I need to change.

DOUG Who reads Joyce? I love Joyce. Who collects stuffed
animals? *(DAPHNE hurries out from the bedroom into the living room,
closing the bedroom door behind her. Behind the door)* Who closed
the door? *(DAPHNE frantically starts changing her clothes. Behind
the door, to COURTNEY)* I'll wait out there till you're ready? *(He
hurries out of the bedroom, closing the door behind him, sees DAPHNE
undressed, stands frozen.)* I don't have any sisters but my cousins
are girls?

(DAPHNE goes into the living-room closet, closes the door. DOUG paces.)

DAPHNE *(From the closet)* You've got me in short sleeves.

COURTNEY *(From the room)* It's still summer.

DAPHNE *(From the closet)* I hate my arms.

COURTNEY *(From the room)* Your arms are great.

DOUG My birthday is September 15? *(There's a knock on the main
door. To himself)* Here he is to tag along on my date.

(He charges to the bedroom door, knocks.)

COURTNEY AND DAPHNE *(From bedroom and closet)* Come in.

*(DOUG slips into the bedroom, closing the door behind him. MICHAEL enters
the living room, closing the door behind him. DAPHNE steps out of the closet
dressed in black.)*

DAPHNE Fifth-choice parents on a ninth-choice planet. I love what
you said. I'd been, wrestling with, something, and the minute
you said it I thought, That's it. *(No response from MICHAEL.)* We

don't choose our parents. We don't choose our planet. *(No response.)* So there's this . . . odd . . .

MICHAEL Actually I'm very close with my parents.

DAPHNE Yeah.

MICHAEL I visit my dad. He's gotten it together.

DAPHNE Right.

MICHAEL I laugh with his wife. I tickle their babies.

DAPHNE Right.

MICHAEL I drop in on Mom. Say hi to her husband. Keep up with his kids. Say hi to my brothers.

DAPHNE Yeah.

MICHAEL I'm back in touch with Mom's ex. My sister stays in his basement.

DAPHNE Uh-huh. But I mean, this sort of—

MICHAEL I'm very close with this planet too.

DAPHNE Right.

MICHAEL Air. Water. Great location.

DAPHNE Right.

MICHAEL Me and my planet, two heaps of shit going in circles.

DAPHNE But moving in here, you feel this sort of—*(A sudden sound from inside the bedroom.)* You know, because it's all so—*(From the bedroom, sounds of bed rocking. Gasps, groans, grunts. Silence.)* It's all sort of—(COURTNEY *rushes out, wrapped in a towel, hurries through the living room and out the main door. Sound of running water in the bathroom.)* I . . . (DOUG *rushes out, wrapped in a towel, hurries through the living room and out the main door. Sound of running water in the bathroom.)* I . . .

(COURTNEY *charges back through the main door, into the bedroom, closing the doors behind her.* DOUG *charges back through the main door, into the bedroom, closing the doors behind him.* DAPHNE *charges into the closet.*

MICHAEL *sits there.* DOUG *comes out from the bedroom, disheveled, despondent, closes the door behind him, sits.*)

DOUG No one here knows my high-school hike club scaled four peaks, I led the way, I won a prize. No one here knows I sprained my foot in a snake pit, kept right on going, everybody cheered and elected me president. No one here knows the feeling, your boots in the dirt, your face in the wind, your picture in the paper. What a gang, what a time, no one knows.

MICHAEL About ready to head to the picnic?

DOUG I might have a prior commitment.

MICHAEL If you had a prior commitment, you'd already know.

DOUG She'll be right out, to let me know.

MICHAEL If you want her to want you, don't let her catch you waiting for her.

DOUG *(Looks at the bedroom door, thinks.)* Huh.

MICHAEL You might also want to go for some deodorant.

DOUG I go for plenty of deodorant.

MICHAEL Go for more.

DOUG *(Sniffs himself, thinks.)* Huh.

MICHAEL Let's head up to the room. I'll do course cards, you call about your lab course . . .

DOUG Why are you telling me to call about my lab course?

MICHAEL To see if you're in.

DOUG I did see. I'm . . . almost in.

MICHAEL Almost in?

DOUG If someone drops out, I'm in.

MICHAEL Oh.

DOUG *(Suddenly incensed)* Excuse me but I'm proud of being almost in? Okay "almost in" is a key step toward being in? Okay I'm sorry I'm not as "in" as you think humanly necessary but not everybody was born into a nationally ranked program that basically guarantees advanced standing?, but at least I'm sticking out my neck instead of dreaming about some graduate-level seminar while fiddling with my goddamn course cards?

(DOUG *charges out the main door.* DAPHNE *steps out from the closet.*)

DAPHNE *(To* MICHAEL*)* I'm heading out if you want to come . . .

(COURTNEY *comes out of the bedroom.*)

COURTNEY If I joined you two, would that be okay?

DAPHNE Might it not be not okay for you?

COURTNEY It'll be great for me, as long as it's okay with you.

DAPHNE But, might you not, see something better, and feel tied?

COURTNEY No.

DAPHNE But aren't you always keeping an eye out, for, you know, whatever, whatever else?

COURTNEY When things happen, things happen, but I never lose sight of my friends. How can you say that?

DAPHNE I meant that crate to be for my books, so why is it covered with your candles?

COURTNEY When you tacitly approve of someone's candles on your crate while secretly resenting them, you're not doing the person a favor.

(DOUG *enters with flowers.*)

DOUG *(To* COURTNEY*)* What was I doing standing in the flowers being stared at like I was crazy by the people I'd been talking with almost happily till the wind shifted and filled me with this feeling of your hair that swept fingers to flowers and feet to stairs to invite you to join me, please join me?

COURTNEY I'm so sorry, but my roommate and I are in the middle of a conversation.

DAPHNE *(To* MICHAEL*)* Weren't *we* in the middle of a conversation?

DOUG Where's the goddamned iced tea?

COURTNEY It's empty.

DOUG I want another crack at it, just one more crack.

COURTNEY I'm sorry.

(The phone starts ringing.)

DOUG I'll recenter your couch. I'll flip it around. I'll stand it on its legs.

COURTNEY I'm sorry.

DOUG Did I only *dream* you wanted to go to the picnic with me? *(To DAPHNE)* If you had other plans, what happened to them?

DAPHNE *(Not moving.)* I'm going to take a nap.

COURTNEY *(To MICHAEL)* Have you any idea how absolutely rude it is to sit there, as though we're not worth one syllable of your divine wisdom?

(DAPHNE picks up the receiver.)

DAPHNE Oh, hi. Right. *(Pause.)* Right. *(Pause. She hangs up.)* My father died.

(Everybody stands there. Blackout.)

Twenty-four Years

2000

>LESLIE AYVAZIAN

ORIGINAL PRODUCTION

DIRECTOR Curt Dempster
ASSISTANT DIRECTOR Nina Steiger
SET DESIGNER Warren Karp
COSTUME DESIGNER Amela Baksic
SOUND Beatrice Terry
PROPS Cynthia Franks
PRODUCTION STAGE MANAGER John Thornberry
STAGE MANAGER Paul Powell

The cast was as follows:
WIFE Leslie Ayvazian
HUSBAND Victor Slezak

CHARACTERS

WIFE

HUSBAND

TIME

The present, evening

A living room. A couch. Music plays. A middle-aged woman stands behind the couch. She holds a glass of champagne. A middle-aged man is seated on the couch. One of his legs is elevated. His knee is bandaged.

HUSBAND Do you want to dance?

WIFE Dance?

HUSBAND Or sway? Do you want to sway with me?

WIFE You think you can do that?

HUSBAND I think I can.

WIFE Okay.

HUSBAND Good. *(He offers her his hand.)*

WIFE One, two, three. No wait, both hands. One, two, three. Okay!

HUSBAND *(Stands.)* Okay!

WIFE You want to lean on me?

HUSBAND I think I'm okay. Let's . . . dance.

(They sway. Tears roll down her cheeks.)

WIFE You okay?

HUSBAND Yeah. Are you okay?

WIFE Yeah. I'm feeling you. I'm holding you.

HUSBAND Hmmm.

ENSEMBLE STUDIO THEATRE MARATHON 2000

(They sway.)

WIFE You want to sit down? You need to sit down?

HUSBAND No. Do you?

WIFE No. *(They sway.)* You feel warm.

HUSBAND No, I don't.

WIFE Do you have a fever?

HUSBAND No.

(She touches his forehead.)

WIFE No, you don't.

HUSBAND See. I was right. I don't have a fever. *(WIFE sniffs.)* So you don't have to worry. *(WIFE sniffs.)* You can say, "Happy anniversary, honey."

WIFE Happy anniversary, honey.

HUSBAND And you can say, "I love you more than ever, even though you have a limp."

WIFE *(Sniffs.)* I need a Kleenex.

HUSBAND Okay.

WIFE They're over there. Come with me. Okay?

HUSBAND Okay. Go.

(They walk together. He limps.)

WIFE AND HUSBAND *(As they walk)* Okay? Okay. Okay? Okay. Okay? Okay.

WIFE Okay. *(Gets Kleenex and blows her nose.)* Twenty-four years. *(She looks over her shoulder at him.)* Hi.

HUSBAND Hi.

WIFE You were so young.

HUSBAND I was twenty-three. You were twenty-eight.

WIFE You gave me your word.

HUSBAND I did.

WIFE *(Blows her nose.)* So young. *(Sniffs.)* And you had that lively girlfriend from Ireland.

HUSBAND Yup. Mary Boyle.

WIFE Mary Boyle, Mary Boyle. She joined the Peace Corps and went to Africa and married that other Peace Corps person. Remember that story she told us about that man in her village who walked around naked with a long string tied to his penis?

HUSBAND Yeah, that guy. And the string had a rock at the end of it. Didn't it? Remember that?

WIFE Mm-hm. He walked around every day dragging that rock from his penis.

(Beat while they think of him.)

HUSBAND Eeeeh.

WIFE Do you want to sit down?

HUSBAND I think I do.

WIFE Does your knee hurt?

HUSBAND It needs a rest.

WIFE You want some aspirin?

HUSBAND I took some.

WIFE You need me to do anything?

HUSBAND Relax. That's not a criticism.

WIFE It's not?

HUSBAND No.

WIFE Okay.

HUSBAND So. Any other romantic memories you want to roll out?

WIFE Um. Well. Do you want to raise anything?

HUSBAND Raise anything? You mean besides this glass?

WIFE Do you want to say anything?

HUSBAND Thank you for keeping your hair long.

WIFE You're welcome. Remember when I cut it all off with a pair of blunt-ended scissors? All the way down to here. *(Indicates hair one inch long.)*

HUSBAND I do.

WIFE I was having that little breakdown.

HUSBAND Yes. You hid in the closet when I came home.

WIFE Oh! You know what I found in the closet?

HUSBAND My gray wool hat?

WIFE Your gray wool hat?

HUSBAND Yeah.

WIFE You left that hat in a taxi.

HUSBAND I know. I just thought you found it.

WIFE You left it in a taxi.

HUSBAND I thought maybe you found it.

WIFE You left that hat in a taxi.

HUSBAND Okay. So what did you find?

WIFE Remember that Christmas gift you bought for my father?

HUSBAND The ceramic knife!

WIFE It was in the closet!

HUSBAND That's a great knife.

WIFE Should we keep it?

HUSBAND I told him about it.

WIFE Maybe he forgot.

HUSBAND He hasn't.

WIFE No. Remember after I cut off my hair into that not-quite-scamp hairdo, you had that flirtation with that girl in the studio?

HUSBAND Yeah.

WIFE And I walked in and stood in the middle of your gazes.

HUSBAND Rosalind.

WIFE Rosalind.

HUSBAND Nothing happened.

WIFE Never kissed?

HUSBAND Never. We never kissed.

WIFE Do you want a pillow under your knee?

HUSBAND No. Thank you. It's fine. I don't need anything.

WIFE All right.

HUSBAND I'm feeling better.

WIFE Okay. What about that Greek guy?

HUSBAND You mean that Greek guy in Greece?

WIFE Yes.

HUSBAND You want me to ask you about him?

WIFE Do you want to?

HUSBAND He followed you to the beach.

WIFE Yes.

HUSBAND He was a jeweler. He showed you some opals. Something about opals.

WIFE He held them in his hands.

HUSBAND Right. And you liked his hands.

WIFE He had nice hands. He was a jeweler.

HUSBAND And he made you a ring.

WIFE He did.

HUSBAND I know nothing happened.

WIFE How do you know?

HUSBAND Because you told me.

WIFE (*Sniffs.*) Right. How's your knee?

HUSBAND It's . . . Honey, it's not your fault that I tore my ligament. (WIFE *sniffs.*) It happens when you play soccer. It happens to lots of people.

WIFE It happened because you didn't have time to warm up.

HUSBAND Maybe. Maybe not.

WIFE And you didn't have time to warm up because I made you late to the game because I asked you not to play that night. I asked you to stay home. I made you late.

HUSBAND It's okay. It is.

WIFE I'm sorry that you tore your ligament. I'm sorry that you had to have surgery. I'm sorry that you are in pain. And I'm so pissed off at you.

HUSBAND I know.

WIFE Why do you have to play soccer at eleven at night, number one?

HUSBAND It's the only time we can get the field.

WIFE Don't answer. I don't want you to answer.

HUSBAND Okay.

WIFE Number two: I had asked you not to play that night because I was afraid of the tests I was getting the next morning. But you said the team needed you, and you walked out the door with your whistle around your neck, while I stood holding the laundry at the top of the stairs. And then . . .

HUSBAND I didn't know.

WIFE What?

HUSBAND You get a lot of tests!

WIFE I have to get a lot of tests! I'm at the age where I have to get a lot of tests! And they make me nervous. And I asked you to stay home that one night. And you left! And then you came home with your knee the size of a watermelon and you snuck into bed while I was sleeping.

HUSBAND I didn't want to wake you.

WIFE I don't think that was your thinking!

HUSBAND Probably not.

WIFE And then you tried to go to work the next morning, but you couldn't walk. And you couldn't walk for one month . . .

HUSBAND I couldn't walk for three weeks.

WIFE It was three weeks and three days. Please. Please!

HUSBAND Okay.

WIFE You couldn't walk for three weeks and three days as we waited for the swelling to go down so you could have the surgery. And then you had the surgery. And you were fully informed about the procedure. And you were awake and inquisitive throughout the operation. And everyone wheeled you into the recovery room in such good humor: the nurses, the surgeon, the anesthesiologist. They all enjoyed the operation, they told me, when I was summoned from the waiting room, which was a far less cheerful atmosphere. And then you came home. And you couldn't move. And you needed everything. And I want to provide you with everything. You want the pen, I get you the pen, you say thank you but not *that* pen, the *other* pen, and I get the other pen, and somehow that's not right either, but you say okay and you're grateful and I want you to be happy. But you are a very particular man. You have very particular needs. And I want to meet them, I do. But do you remember that I *had asked you not to go out that night? Do you remember that? Do you remember?*

HUSBAND Yes.

WIFE *And? And? And?*

HUSBAND And I'm sorry. I'm sorry I went the way I went.

WIFE And yes?

HUSBAND And I intended to leave the game early, but we were short a man and I'm the coach and . . .

WIFE You're the coach, I know. I know you were voted the coach.

HUSBAND I wasn't voted coach. I volunteered.

WIFE You volunteered!

HUSBAND No one else wanted to do it.

WIFE Okay. You volunteered to be the coach. And you were attentive and prompt, and you brought cold sodas to every game.

HUSBAND I wasn't the only one to bring sodas. Sometimes others did as well.

WIFE Sometimes others did as well, but mostly you.

HUSBAND No, others brought . . .

WIFE No no no, mostly you! You you you! I know that's true.

HUSBAND Okay. I brought more sodas than other people. And I wore the whistle. I was the coach.

WIFE Yes, yes. Coach. Yes. That's the way you are.

HUSBAND Yes, it is.

WIFE And on that night, when I was feeling frightened and asked you please to stay home, you went to the game! And now you are *enfeebled*.

HUSBAND It's not permanent. I won't always be enfeebled.

WIFE Maybe a year.

HUSBAND Maybe less.

WIFE With tons of physical therapy.

HUSBAND I can do that. I can do that.

WIFE Ohhhh.

HUSBAND Honey, I will be spry again.

(Beat.)

WIFE Tell me the things you will do when you're spry.

HUSBAND I will get my own pens. And I will hold you . . . next to me.

WIFE And here it is our twenty-fourth anniversary.

HUSBAND Yep. We're middle-aged.

WIFE I'm more middle-aged. And you're enfeebled.

HUSBAND Right. I'm . . . um . . . I'm sorry this has been hard for you.

WIFE No, shhh, shut up.

HUSBAND I know you're sick of this.

WIFE No, stop, don't apologize . . . don't. *(Beat.)* Have you noted that you have been with me for more than half your life?

HUSBAND I have. You courted me.

WIFE I did.

HUSBAND You sent me flowers. You bought me that desk.

WIFE That desk. That huge desk. Delivered to your sublet apartment.

HUSBAND The big desk in the small place.

WIFE It was nice.

HUSBAND It was.

WIFE Then I proposed to you.

HUSBAND Mm-hm.

WIFE And you said no.

HUSBAND So you asked again.

WIFE One week later.

HUSBAND And I said yes.

WIFE I seduced you.

HUSBAND You did.

WIFE Do you think I tricked you? Deceived you?

HUSBAND No.

WIFE Vamped you?

HUSBAND No. Vamped?

WIFE Ya.

HUSBAND Okay, yes. You vamped me. I was vamped.

WIFE Fine. Shove over.

HUSBAND What?

WIFE Just move your leg over in that direction. Just move it. Come on. Move it!

HUSBAND Okay, sure. I'll lift my injured, throbbing leg and move it over here. *(He does.)*

WIFE Good. *(She sits close to him. Beat.)* You feel warm.

HUSBAND No, I don't.

WIFE You're okay?

HUSBAND I am.

WIFE You need anything?

HUSBAND I need you to kiss my knee.

WIFE *(Not moving.)* So I have to get up?

HUSBAND No! I wouldn't want you to do anything you don't want to do!

(She kisses his knee.)

WIFE Is it better?

HUSBAND . . . Yup.

(She pats his knee.)

WIFE With this knee, I thee wed.

(Beat.)

HUSBAND With all that I am . . .

WIFE With all that I am.

HUSBAND And all that I have . . .

WIFE Uh-huh.

HUSBAND I honor you. From this day forward . . .

WIFE Until we are parted . . .

BOTH By death.

HUSBAND This is my solemn vow.

WIFE Mine too. *(Beat.)* Did you look that up?

HUSBAND No.

WIFE You remembered it?

HUSBAND Yes.

WIFE Did you get me a present?

HUSBAND No.

WIFE Me neither.

(Lights out.)

The Seventeenth of June

2000

> EDWARD ALLAN BAKER

ORIGINAL PRODUCTION

DIRECTOR Jamie Richards
SET DESIGNER Chris Jones
COSTUME DESIGNER Julie Doyle
SOUND Robert Gould
PROPS Laura Raynor
PRODUCTION STAGE MANAGER Jim Ring
STAGE MANAGER Rachel Putnam

The cast was as follows:
DEE Fiona Gallagher
CHET Joseph Lyle Taylor
KAT Geneva Carr
PATRICE Ellen Mareneck

CHARACTERS

DEE thirty
CHET thirty-five, a plain-looking man
KAT late twenties
PATRICE thirty-five-ish

PLACE

East Providence, Rhode Island

TIME

Summer, 1999

This play is dedicated to the memory of the actress Billie Neal.

PRE-SHOW MUSIC

Blues

The kitchen of a third-floor apartment. The room is empty except for a table and some chairs, arranged center stage.

Lights up on DEE *staring down at a chalk outline of a body drawn on a dining-room table while Nina Simone's recording of "My Man's Gone Now" plays from a cassette player.* DEE *is wearing a long black dress over her jeans. She strokes the table in a loving manner. Sings some. Is sad some. She lays her body atop the table. Closes her eyes. Music plays on. Behind her against the wall is* KAT *eating a doughnut, drinking coffee, and watching* DEE *as if she's viewing* TV. *A few feet from* KAT *is* CHET *in pressed slacks, a long-sleeved shirt (buttoned to the top), and shiny shoes. He watches* DEE *with an air of emotional detachment. A half dozen empty Dunkin' Donuts boxes are scattered about, along with empty coffee cups and pizza boxes. Cleaning stuff crowds the counter, and a broom, pail, and mop are in a corner of the room.*

Pause.

Enter PATRICE *with a box of stuff in her arms. She wears skintight slacks, a tight summery top, sunglasses. She takes in the situation.*

PATRICE Oh Christ . . . *(She drops the box. Turns off the music.)* I'd say three days is about enough a this shit.

KAT Poor thing. Breaks my heart to see her like this.

PATRICE Yeah, that's sweet, but she's gotta go—like now. I just signed the lease to this place, I got the U-Haul packed and parked on the street—and . . . *(Goes to* DEE *at the table.)* C'mon, Dee—this was interesting for a coupla days, but now it's just a little too much blood in the water, you know what I'm saying?

Little too much salt on the fries, okay, just a little too much sugar in the coffee, so you gotta snap outta this retarded behavior, change your clothes, have your boyfriend here take you out for some meat and salad, then go back to work at the nursin' home asking the old broads if they want green or yellow Jell-O today. Ant is history, okay, he almost killed you, he abused you, he lived to fuck you over, his purpose in life was to fuck you over. Now, granted you two were a couple for a long time—why, none of us have a fucking clue—but that was between you two, and I understand how sometimes a man's bad side can be—how should I say, uh—

KAT Sexy?

PATRICE No, not sexy.

DEE How can you say all that to me?! How can you forget your brother-in-law so fast?!

KAT I haven't forgotten him, Dee.

DEE It's not up to you to tell me when to stop mourning for him!

PATRICE Go mourn someplace else is all I'm sayin'! I got new goals to meet, a new life to live, a truck I'm payin' for by the hour, so c'mon, chop, chop, the "new me" is burstin' at the seams!

DEE Ant is dead! I'll never see 'im again! Ant is dead!

PATRICE Dee is alive! Dee moves on! Dee is alive!

DEE I go away . . . for two days I go away and—

CHET *(Clears his throat.)* We go away.

DEE —and Ant in this very room—at this very table—with our favorite "mix of love songs" playing over and over, and I imagine such pain—

PATRICE Can I cut in here?

DEE —and all the pain was—was too big for his heart—

PATRICE Dee, sister, don't take me through this again—

DEE —the pain moved up up up up from his heart to his throat— then—it settled in his esophagus—

KAT I'm going to cry . . .

DEE It—the pain a me not bein' here—got stuck in his esophagus and it was too big—

PATRICE *(Quickly)* "and his esophagus veins were too small and so they burst open."

DEE And his esophagus veins were too small and so they burst open . . . *(She collapses on the table.)*

PATRICE Oh shit . . .

KAT *(Goes to* DEE.*)* Dee? You want me to go out for more doughnuts? How 'bout a Heath bar? Some perfume? To take your mind off a this sad sad day—

PATRICE Kat, back off! And stop with the 'sad sad day" shit, okay. You're not helping the situation, and—

DEE *(Cuts her off.)* He's gone. No more Ant. It all comes down to a chalk outline of his body at the table where he first slapped me.

PATRICE Then *take* the fucking table! *Sleep* with the fucking table! *Eat* the fucking table! *Burn* the fucking table!

DEE I was sitting there, and he was sitting there—it was soon after we got married and he was pretending to read the paper. He didn't know I knew he couldn't read, so I says to him, "I know you can't read and it's okay, Ant, 'cause I love you," and he leaned in, and I thought he was going to kiss me, but I—I got slapped instead, and he said, "Readin' isn't important now that people can get a hundred channels." I sat there, right there, hurt, listening to the TV—

PATRICE That's a good memory?

KAT You know he was kinda right about that—

PATRICE That's enough, Kat—

CHET *(Finally)* Dee . . . I miss you . . .

PATRICE Good, good thing to say, Chet, and let's not forget, my dear sister Dee, that you were away from Ant for two months, okay, two months you lived downstairs with this nice man who took you in, fed you, listened to you, and what else did you do, Chet? Help me here.

CHET Well um, Scrabble. Parcheesi. Gin rummy. Fed my fish. Played with my bird. Watched TV. We ate, of course. Cleaned. Up at six. In bed by ten.

DEE Ant died alone—goddamn it—prob'ly crying out my name— and where was I? Huh? Where was I?

CHET You were with me in front of a slot machine at the Indian casino.

DEE *Exactly!*

CHET Dee, I care so much for you—

DEE With a handful of quarters I'm screaming, "Three lemons, come on!" And Ant's here—dying—alone . . .

PATRICE All right, all right, okay, okay, I'm at the fork in the road and it's ninety-five fucking degrees and I'm a minute away from totally losing it even *before* dealing with you and this shit. I mean, I didn't tell you, but the last time Kevin threw me off our houseboat I almost fucking drowned—but I got to the top, and while I was bobbing up and down with the Coke and beer cans all around me—I thought, "This is it, this is fucking it, no more putting up with a man who makes me sink below my worth because I'm afraid to be alone."

KAT What was the reason he threw you over this time?

PATRICE He was fasting.

KAT Oh, so he gets moody.

PATRICE Skinny bastard turns into this, this insect, and—

DEE *(Cuts her off.)* How could you live here? Knowing Ant died in this room, how could you live here?

KAT I couldn't.

PATRICE The "old Patrice" couldn't, but the "new Patrice" can.

KAT I couldn't.

PATRICE Once I move in here and get his smell out, I'm going to look into starting my own business, okay. "Scented clothing." A lilac dress will smell like lilacs, an orange T-shirt will smell like an orange, a blue—

KAT What will something white smell like?

DEE *(Suddenly)* The *guilt* I have . . . I'm sick to my heart with—

PATRICE *(Cuts her off.)* Dee, he had the guilt, not you. I mean, he didn't even leave you a note and you're—

DEE *(Cuts her off.)* He did leave a note. I could hardly read his kindergarten handwriting, but—it's so sad—(*She hands* PATRICE *a piece of paper.*)

PATRICE *(Reads aloud.)* "Wish . . . I wasn't . . . born . . . in Portugal."

DEE Broke my heart.

PATRICE Yeah . . . tears are rolling down my face.

KAT His veins must've burst before he could finish, cause that makes no sense—even to me.

CHET *(Rises.)* Dee, what are we going to do? Huh? What? Me and your sisters moved all of Ant's stuff and furniture down into my apartment. I haven't been to my job in three days, and . . .

KAT What do you do, Chet?

CHET Computer salvage work.

PATRICE I can see that . . .

KAT What's a computer savage?

PATRICE Sal-vage. He saves what can be reused.

CHET *(Continues with* DEE.*)* I been here the whole time—watching, caring, gagging sometimes, but most of all hoping you'll pop up, look around, and say, "What the heck am I doing? How did I end up back up here?" You'll turn around and see goofy me and remember all the stuff we talked about the nights you were downstairs with me, and how we spent hours listening to Ant pacing up here like a dog in heat in the night's heat. You'd snuggle closer to me, happy to be not here. You told me I saved your life. I told you, "It was by accident." You told me I brought out something in you not felt before. I told you the same goes for me. *(Pause. He sits at the table. Looks at* DEE.*)* We found each other on the back stairway of this building. That day . . . I saw you huddled on the steps is a day I remember in vivid detail. The amount of breaths you took. Your hair all over the place. One eye was swollen shut. Dress was ripped down from your left shoulder. Lips were puffy. One cheek was up against the kid-smudged wall, and you said—

DEE *(Interrupts.)* What day is it today?

CHET It's the seventeenth of June.

(Lights soften some.)

DEE *(Softly)* It's my thirtieth birthday.

CHET Happy birthday.

DEE I'm Dee.

CHET Chet.

DEE I'm not doing too good today.

CHET I know.

DEE I guess I—I got beat up some.

CHET I'm sorry.

DEE He's dying. Has bad days. Bad nights.

CHET I live under you.

DEE Oh. Then you heard.

CHET I heard.

DEE (Pause.) Your name's Chet?

CHET Chet, yeah.

DEE I'm Dee.

CHET And today you're thirty.

DEE I—I don't remember what we were fighting about . . . um . . .

CHET That's okay.

DEE Well, I made it. To thirty, anyway.

CHET That's good.

DEE I'm embarrassed.

CHET Why?

DEE 'Cause you know what goes on.

CHET Don't be embarrassed.

DEE I'm ashamed.

CHET Don't be ashamed.

DEE You prob'ly think I'm a cheap welfare type who deserves what I get, right?

CHET God, no. My mother and father used to fight all the—

DEE I can't get away from him, you know that, right?

CHET Why?

DEE What?

CHET Why can't you get away from him?

DEE I . . . um . . .

CHET Don't you want to?

DEE I can't . . . I can't break away . . . I . . . you know, last night he said to me, "Without you I'm as good as empty and dead."

CHET Uh-huh.

DEE "Empty and dead without you . . ." What am I sayin' . . . You don't look like the type who . . . um . . .

CHET Knows what you're talking about?

DEE You don't look the type.

CHET When I was a kid, I . . . *(Beat.)*

DEE Oh. Sorry.

CHET I . . . uh . . . couldn't help her. My mother . . .

DEE *(After a beat.)* I'm his wife. I can't let him . . . just . . .

CHET He hurts you . . .

DEE Die.

CHET What?

DEE I can't let him . . . die. I can't let him die.

(Beat. Lights come back up.)

CHET Then you passed out and I . . . I picked you up in my arms—

DEE And I woke up in your mother's bed the next day. Tea and toast on a tray next to me.

KAT *(After a beat.)* I'm so sorry I didn't get in touch with you that day, Dee, but that was the day I got the concussion from falling off a city bus, and it's a funny story that involves this deaf

Chinese woman, but anyway—oh God, what a confusing day that was . . . Yup, the seventeenth of June was the day that happened.

PATRICE *(To* DEE*)* And while we're on that day, I'm sorry I didn't call you or return your call. It sounded like you needed me, but . . . I'll make it up next year.

DEE I don't remember callin' anybody, um . . .

KAT Left me a message, too, but I was dizzy all day.

CHET Dee . . . c'mon, let's go downstairs.

PATRICE You got a guy who cares for you *and* has a job. Run with it, honey, and don't look back.

DEE I . . . I . . . can't . . . move . . . out of this . . .

PATRICE Chet, pick her up like you did two months ago and carry her downstairs.

DEE Leave me alone. Please. Just leave me alone.

CHET Is that what you really want? Huh? Is it? Is that the gosh darn truth?

DEE Yes! *I want to be left alone!*

PATRICE Well, you can't do it here 'cause it's costing me money, so c'mon, Dee, snap outta this like *fast*!

KAT And if I could have the keys to Ant's Camaro before this gets any crazier.

CHET *(To* DEE*)* So now I have to sit and look and wait for the grieving widow and accept that everything *we* did and said together downstairs was—was what?

DEE I was confused when you took me in—I liked the break from my life up here, and it was . . . um . . . a comfort to be with you, and to live without him knowing where I was, but—

CHET He knew you were with me.

DEE What?

PATRICE What did you just say, Chet?

DEE Chet, what did you just say?

KAT He said Ant knew you were with Chet.

CHET He and I talked.

DEE He knew the whole time?!

CHET Yes yes, one time I was taking out the trash, and you were at work, and he captured me, brought me up here and told me he knew you were at my place but he was going to allow it to happen because he wanted to change before he died. He wanted to withdraw from you before he died. So he asked me to help him, and if I did—he would allow you to stay with me. I only had to help him become a nice person, and teach him to read and write.

DEE I don't believe this . . .

CHET We spent early morning and late nights together. Talking. He told me from the day he first saw you he wanted to own you, that with you on his arm it made him seem better than he really was, and when you were out of his sight he went mad inside imagining you flirting with every man you came in contact with.

DEE *(Stares at him; then)* Ant knowing I was with you, and not coming to get me is like—way, way the fuck out there!

CHET I'm not done.

PATRICE Oh God . . .

KAT I just need the keys to the Camaro, then—

CHET *(Interrupts.)* Last weekend—Ant pushed death's card.

DEE And that means . . . what?

CHET He planned it. He knew how bad those veins were. He was told not to exercise. You know that. So he—last weekend— told me to take you to the casino—then he worked out. Did push-ups—as many as it would take.

DEE So—he "pushed up" to death?

CHET That was his plan.

PATRICE You're freaking me out a little here, Chet.

CHET He told me everything—from day one.

KAT Like—from the day he was born?

CHET From the first thing he remembers.

KAT In Portugal?

CHET Forget Portugal! That was only the first sentence he ever wrote. He was proud of it.

PATRICE Wait a minute, he told you everything?

KAT I really should go.

CHET I have all the answers to why he did certain things at certain times in specific detail, all from his perspective.

KAT His what?

PATRICE His view.

KAT His view of what?

PATRICE Her! Dee!

CHET I know—what it feels like to hit you. I know what it feels like to watch you spit up blood. And I know what it feels like to watch you clean it up, crying all the while.

KAT *(Moves to* CHET.*)* Poor Chet . . .

CHET I can tell you about Ant—and Kat, and their late-night phone calls.

KAT Oh shit, Chet . . .

CHET How he soothed her.

KAT Well . . . um . . . okay, soothed is about . . . um . . . right . . .

PATRICE Kat—I don't believe it.

KAT A few phone calls, big deal, so he soothed me; arrest me if that's wrong!

PATRICE You, Kat, doing the dirty-phone-call dance with Ant?!

KAT It wasn't dirty!

CHET He was gentle with her.

KAT And gentle is good, goddamn it!

DEE I can't believe what's going on here!

CHET *(To* KAT*)* Should I go on?

KAT If you do I'm going to contort into this strange position, and you're all going to laugh.

DEE Kat, I'm stunned at this—this stuff I'm hearing, and you're saying it's true?

KAT He—he was nice to me. Said nice things to me, and I forgot everything and anything that happened in the dark—in my past. He—he told me not to be ashamed of my body, and that I shouldn't be feeling shame at all—'cause he knew . . . the time that thing happened to me that long, long time ago . . . um . . . so he—he said, "Kat, you're a special person, and never, never let anyone take away your dignity, and from now until ever I will be your angel. I will be outside every window, in every room you enter, and I will make sure—"

PATRICE AND KAT "—that every breath you take is without tiredness, unrest, anger, and memory, so—"

PATRICE, KAT, AND CHET "Starting now and lasting forever—no one will ever hurt you again."

*(*DEE *stares at the three of them in utter disbelief.)*

CHET I helped him with that.

DEE So—the *three of you* were . . . ?!

PATRICE Ant and I did talk . . . but we didn't get into your shit, okay, it was about me. My life.

KAT Same with me.

PATRICE He never wandered.

KAT True in my case, too.

PATRICE And it started, oh, I don't know, week or so after the seventeenth of June. Saw him. He was all nice and . . .

KAT That's true in my case, too.

CHET Dee, he let me in. I let him in.

PATRICE And just for the record, me and Ant never did "it." We'd meet at the Hitching Post Motel and . . . um . . . talk. And he would give me a massage—a long one, neck, back mostly—he'd stroke my back like a mountain lion without claws, hardly pressing down at all with the flat of his hand, he'd start with the neck, then go all the way down—down . . . down . . . down . . .

(Silence.)

KAT Oooh, I just got a chill—

PATRICE "Cry, Patrice, cry out all the tears you been holding in . . . Get out all that shit about never being loved . . . never being loved the way you dream about, and never being who you really want to be . . . so come on, start seeing that new person, start hearing that new person." He'd stroke . . . one hand after the other . . . "You hear her? Sssh, listen for her, sssh, listen . . ." *(Beat.)* Well, I didn't . . . not until I almost drowned.

(PATRICE stares down at the chalk outline of Ant's body. KAT comes up beside her and looks down at the table. It's like they're looking at Ant in a coffin. DEE is in some kind of shock, staring at them.)

KAT He gave me someone who understood, someone who made me laugh until I cried; someone, a man I felt I could trust. And he told me something I will never ever ever forget. *(Beat.)* "Kat, my Camaro is yours."

PATRICE For me it was "The security deposit on my apartment can be your security deposit."

DEE *What are you three doing to me?!*

CHET Telling you the truth. He wanted us to keep it from you, but—

PATRICE But it's out, and I got a truck of my past belongings ready to be moved and sorted out, so let's—

KAT And if you could get me the keys to his—

DEE *(Cuts her off.)* He's torturing me from the grave 'cause I—I left him to die alone, that's what this is! He used you to get to me! He played with the three of you!

CHET No no. He and I became friends . . . uh . . . we talked a lot about him, and I told him everything about me and how I cared for my mother until she . . . until . . . sorry, I can't say it . . .

KAT Can't say what?

PATRICE That his mother's dead.

CHET That giving up some part of my life for her made me soft inside, but I had to. Ant helped me be more forceful in terms of getting things that I want.

DEE Okay, okay, you *have* to stop this—it's time to *stop*!

CHET Dee, he told me the thing that hurt him the most in the end is that he saw that young girl he was in love with disappear—

DEE I knew Ant for half my life and I never heard him talk that way! Never!

CHET Right, right, you just saw and heard the old Ant, the man who if he was in this situation would be like—"All right, bitch, you fucking cut it out right here, and I don't wanna hear any back talk, 'cause I've had enough of your—your—" whatever profanity Ant would say there, and . . . uh . . .

KAT *(Cuts him off.)* Was he just being Ant?

PATRICE Wake up, will ya, Kat?

CHET Dee, the point is, the screen is clear, and we know each other. I mean, I know everything about you from what you told me *and* what he told me. We're connected—connected at the soul . . .

(Slight pause.)

PATRICE Say "Yes, we're connected at the soul," and I love you, so let's go downstairs and make love till we're wet in the face!

KAT But before that—"I have to find Ant's car keys for Kat."

CHET It's all in place. The plan that is meant to be. Little bizarre, but interesting. But the bottom line being—we were meant to meet that day on the back staircase—and now two months later, everything is about to take on a different tone and color, starting as soon as you take my hand and walk downstairs with me.

(Silence. Then PATRICE *and* KAT *applaud.)*

PATRICE Nice, nice. Okay, good, good . . .

KAT Very good, very good—

PATRICE So have a nice life and bye-bye—

KAT And if you'll give me the car keys I'll drive you anywhere you want; gas is on me—

DEE Back off! For Chrissakes, you're like Cinderella's evil sisters, back off! Sit over there! *(They do.* DEE *turns to* CHET.*)* Chet?

CHET Dee.

DEE Chet, right? Not Ant.

CHET Um . . . Ant's kinda like on a file. I can bring him up.

DEE And "snap" he's here.

CHET I know him that well.

DEE I'm hatin' this attitude you got, Chet—

CHET I'm sorry—

DEE With all your *"information"*—

CHET I went too far—

DEE "I know your secrets, your pain—"

CHET I never said "I knew your—"

DEE "So think of it as some plan—"

CHET Okay, okay—

DEE I might've had a fucked-up childhood Ant saved me from— but I still got a place inside a me that—

CHET You don't have to do this—

DEE You wanna be Ant?! Fine, c'mon, be Ant, and tell me the day, the exact fucking day we stopped bein' two normal people with normal jobs livin' in a normal neighborhood! And don't blame it on your sickness! I need some answers, goddamn it! Why the fuck would you be hittin' me on my birthday?!

PATRICE Hey, Dee, you all right?

DEE Like you actually care if I'm all right!

PATRICE Whadda you saying?! A course I care!

KAT We both care, Dee—

DEE While you were fallin' for Ant's shit, were you caring?!

PATRICE He helped us, what can we say?!

DEE *And what he did to me didn't fucking matter?!*

PATRICE You were away from him!

DEE I . . . I called you . . . on my birthday, I called you . . . *(Beat.)* "Hey, Patrice, I'm callin' to . . . um . . . to see if you're around 'cause . . . uh—I . . . lately been not . . . um . . . too good and just lookin' to . . . uh . . . I don't know, just wanted to hear your voice . . . have ya make me laugh, and say . . ."

PATRICE Right, right . . .

DEE "I love you . . ."

PATRICE I'm sorry, okay? I had my own shit to deal with and, well, I, I . . . got no excuse, whadda am I saying?

KAT Honest to God, I *was* out of it that day, so I'm kind of hazy on what you said, but I remember you ending with—"I love you . . ."

DEE It's my birthday . . . and nobody's talkin' to me . . .

CHET What did you do after the calls?

DEE I . . .

CHET Look at me, Dee. *(She does.)* You got up, made the calls—

DEE I felt sick—

CHET What did you do *after* the calls?

DEE What?

CHET You got up late the day of the seventeenth—

DEE Sick.

CHET Because of the fight the night before.

DEE I had had it.

CHET Because of the fight the night before.

DEE He said at the end of it—"Without you I'm as good as empty and dead . . ."

CHET So you're up, sick, make the calls.

DEE I was feeling . . .

CHET What? Say it.

DEE I get so little. Have so little.

CHET Where are you?

DEE It's my thirtieth birthday, and I'm thinkin' how my mother put butter on our noses on the morning of our birthday for good luck . . .

CHET Is Ant with you?

DEE Ant?

CHET Where's Ant?

DEE I'm at the counter . . .

CHET Good . . .

DEE The seventeenth of June is always the best weather day of the year . . . Then I . . . I hear him . . . and I . . . I . . .

PATRICE Dee, you okay doing this?

CHET Stay away from her! *(PATRICE backs away.)* Dee, look at me . . .

DEE My back's to him, but I hear him . . . and he says, "What the fuck are you doin'?"

CHET When he got you to face him he saw how sad you looked, saddest he ever saw—

DEE *"Wipe that look off your face,"* he spits.

CHET Inside he hated saying that.

DEE It's my birthday, I can look whatever way I want, asshole!

CHET Inside he was proud to see you stand up to him.

DEE *So, fuck you!*

CHET He slapped you, his ring caught your bottom lip. *"You wanna take me on, is that what you want?!"*

(DEE *runs from* CHET.)

DEE I'm on the . . . the floor lookin' at a spot of tomato sauce I missed cleaning . . . Now, how did I miss that spot?

CHET "Get the fuck up and tell me why you'd do somethin' so crazy . . ."

DEE My hair . . . he has my hair and he's pullin' . . . He, he pulls me up to him . . . to his face—

(CHET *is right up to her.*)

CHET "What the fuck are you trying to prove?!"

DEE Let . . . go . . . of . . . me . . .

KAT Stop this, Patrice!

PATRICE How can I stop it if I don't know what's *really* going on?!

CHET Both of you, just stay over there!

KAT God, feels like being with Mom and Dad twenty years ago. I don't like this.

DEE I remember the beer and smoke taste in our first kiss . . .

CHET He forgot the first kiss.

DEE But after that . . . nothin' I remember. A blank.

CHET He wanted to change his mind but couldn't and punched you with his fist. *"Whadda you goin' mental on me?!"*

DEE Hit again. *(She runs to the table.* CHET *is right with her.)*

CHET Harder than the other.

DEE I—I couldn't see for a few seconds . . .

CHET Inside he wanted to pull you to him, and cry.

DEE *(Faces* CHET.*)* His strong hands wrapped around my throat . . .

CHET Why was he choking you, Dee?

DEE I . . . don't know . . .

CHET There *was* a reason!

DEE *I don't know why!*

CHET You do, Dee, you do!

DEE *There was always a reason!*

CHET But on your birthday, why—

DEE *(Cuts him off.)* "You didn't set the alarm clock." "You didn't cook the meat well enough." "You forgot to change the sheets . . ."

CHET It wasn't any of that—

DEE No . . .

CHET Then what was it?!

DEE "Dee, you forgot to iron my pants!"

CHET No—

DEE "Dee, you're gettin' fat!" "What the fuck are you wearin'?!" "Stop your bitchin'!" "I saw you smilin' at that guy, don't fuckin' lie to me!"

(DEE is taking quick breaths. CHET gets closer to her. She backs up to the counter, turns her back to him.)

CHET *(More forceful)* It's the morning of your birthday, you call your sisters, then you're at the counter thinking about your mother with the butter for—

DEE *(Cuts him off.)* The seventeenth of June is always so . . . and I hear 'im . . . he's . . . he's behind me . . .

CHET What are you doing?!

DEE *(Turns around.)* I have . . . I have the sharpest knife and I'm holding it by two hands facing my stomach, ready to stab hard into my . . . *(Beat.)*

PATRICE Oh my God . . .

KAT You were going to kill yourself . . .

DEE *(In a run-on stream of consciousness)* "What the fuck are you doing?" He—he spins me around. "Wipe that look off of your face!" He grabs the knife, but I won't let go. *It's my birthday, I can look whatever way I want, Asshole!* He takes the knife, throws it . . . *Fuck you.* He slaps me hard, my lip opens up, I fall to the floor. *"You wanna take me on, is that what you want?!?"* He picks me up by the hair. *"Whadda you goin' mental on me?!"* He hits me and hits me, and his hands go around my throat . . . *(She puts her hands around her throat.)* . . . and I see tears like I never saw from him pourin' out, and he's pressin' my throat harder—C'mon, you fuck, I think, press harder, press . . .

CHET   He saw, for the first time, your eyes . . .

DEE   One more squeeze . . .

CHET   With no life.

DEE   I don't feel anythin' . . . nothin' . . . Not his hands on my throat, not the cuts, I feel nothin' . . .

(Beat.)

CHET   What happened? *(Beat.)* What happened next?!

DEE   I . . . I don't know . . . I . . .

CHET   C'mon, what happened next?!

DEE   I don't remember . . .

CHET   Where are his hands, Dee? What happened next?!

DEE   *(Looks at* CHET.*)* He loosened his grip.

CHET   He let up.

DEE   His hands dropped down.

CHET   Took a step back.

DEE   I felt the aches come back—tasted blood—

CHET   He thought, "Today's the day . . . I let her go."

DEE   He tucked his hand under my arm, gentle-like, walked me to the door, opened it, said nothin', then—he put me out. Closed the door, soft . . . then click went the lock. Click. *(Silence. She is in the center of the space. She looks up at her surroundings as if she has just snapped away from a dream. Looks at* CHET. *Softly)* Okay . . . *(Beat.)* Okay . . .

PATRICE Oh Christ, Dee, what's happened to us that we don't run when one of us cries out for help?

KAT The three of us used to be so close, and the thought of one of you gone makes me sick inside, oh shit . . . I feel so ashamed . . .

DEE *(Looks at* CHET.*)* Don't be ashamed. *(After a beat.)* Patrice, start to bring your stuff up, and, Kat, the keys are in the Camaro.

*(*KAT *goes to* DEE.*)*

KAT The whole time?!

*(*PATRICE *goes to* DEE.*)*

PATRICE Oh, calm down, for Chrissakes, you don't even have a license.

KAT Well, the new me is going to get one, so you calm down.

*(*DEE *is between them.)*

PATRICE I'll calm down when I want to calm down.

KAT And you never answered my question "What's a white shirt going to smell like?"

DEE Snow. A white shirt should smell like snow.

PATRICE *(Going along.)* Okay.

KAT Okay.

DEE Remember that smell when we were kids?

KAT I remember the smell of burnin' leaves.

PATRICE For me it's the smell of Dad's Old Spice. *(After a moment the three share an embrace.)* C'mon, Kat, let's leave her alone. I'll teach you to drive the Camaro.

(They start to exit.)

KAT Is it an automatic or a stick?

PATRICE C'mon, it's Ant's car, it's a stick.

(They exit. Silence.)

CHET Let's go downstairs.

DEE Chet . . . I . . . I don't wanna be your mother.

CHET I know, I know.

DEE *(Goes to him.)* You helped me . . . you helped her. Chet . . . you did it.

CHET *(Smiles.)* Yeah.

DEE Now . . . I'd like to be alone.

CHET And then?

DEE Go to the beach. Go for a swim.

CHET You want me to come? I'll buy you some clam cakes and chowder.

DEE *(After a beat.)* Maybe tomorrow.

(After a moment CHET *walks to the door, stops, turns to* DEE.*)*

CHET You know what I heard the other night that made me think of you?

DEE What?

CHET The sound an airplane makes on a windy night.

DEE I love that sound.

CHET You told me.

DEE And I don't know why.

CHET *(Confidently)* I know why.

*(*CHET *exits.* DEE *looks at the door for a moment, then goes to the cassette player to reverse the tape. Pushes Play. She looks around the room as Nina Simone's "Gin House Blues" begins.* DEE *tears off the black dress and tosses it into a corner. She dances over to the sink, wets a sponge, then proceeds to the table and begins washing off the chalk outline of Ani's body as the music increases in volume and the lights begin a slow fade to black.)*

Birth Marks

2000

>LESLIE CAPUTO

ORIGINAL PRODUCTION

DIRECTOR Abigail Zealey Bess
SET DESIGNER Carlo Adinolfi
COSTUME DESIGNER Bruce Goodrich
SOUND Robert Gould
PROPS Laura Raynor
PRODUCTION STAGE MANAGER Jim Ring
STAGE MANAGER Sonda Staley

The cast was as follows:
TERRY Jenna Lamia
YVONNE Nicole Gomez
POP Martin Shakar
LUIS Ramon de Ocampo

CHARACTERS

TERRY seventeen, first generation working-class Irish-American

YVONNE seventeen, Terry's best friend and sister-in-law, Puerto Rican

POP late fifties, Terry's father, Irish

LUIS twenty-one, Yvonne's older brother, Puerto Rican

PLACE

A Catholic hospital located on New York's Lower East Side

TIME

The present, winter

A small maternity ward. There are four beds that run perpendicular against the back wall. Little nightstands separate the beds. The decoration is sterile. The door to the room is downstage left.

Opening music starts at preset. Lights go to black as music continues. At determined crescendo—BANG!—lights go up. Music continues.

TERRY *is sitting up in the only occupied bed in the room, the third from stage right. She is wearing a pink robe over a lace camisole. Tiny-sized jeans are thrown on the floor. She is listening to music on a Walkman. She is reading legal documents when the phone rings, once, twice, three times . . .* TERRY *pulls off her headphones—Music stops. She answers the phone.*

TERRY Hello? Yes? *(Listens.)* I've tried to read it! It's not exactly easy to understand, you know! *(Listens.)* I just don't know yet, okay?! *(Listens.)* Well . . . does that mean I couldn't see her? You never told me if—*(Listens.)* Please! *(Listens.)* Please let me just think about it!!! *(She hangs up the phone hard.)* Shit!

(TERRY goes back to reading the documents. POP, her father, enters. TERRY hides the papers in a magazine on the bed.)

POP You wanna tell me what the deal is with all the nuns in this place? I almost knocked down a little one comin' outta the elevator.

TERRY It's a Catholic hospital. What'ya expect?

POP What are you doin' over there?!

TERRY Nothin'!

POP So, has he come by, then?

TERRY Oh my God, Pop. You're not suppose to be up here. How'd you get past 'em downstairs?

POP Never mind that! I just want a yes or no answer!

TERRY They're not suppose to let anybody up until ten. Some security they got in this place.

POP That's all I'm here for. I'm not here to do anythin' else. Give me the answer, like I don't know what it is already, and I'll take care of business like I gotta.

TERRY Oh, please!

POP Yes or no, Terry?

TERRY Would ya leave me alone already? Let me handle my own life? Would ya? Once? Just stay outta this? Please, Pop? What'ya say?

POP That's a no!

TERRY Pop! Give it a rest! I just had a baby two days ago. What do you want me to do, start hemorrhagin' here?

POP What did I tell ya, huh? What did I say the day you married that bastid?

TERRY I don't wanna talk about this now!

POP I said he was no good, am I right?

TERRY Pop—

POP —I said it would be a bigger mistake than marryin' a nig—

TERRY (*Jumps over him so he can't finish the word.*) Okay!!! Do you know you could get yourself killed talkin' like that? You can't say that word! I told you over and over—someone hears you sayin' that and BANG! you're dead!

POP He's a bum! That's all I'm sayin'.

TERRY Why are you torturin' me?

POP You're gonna have to wake up to the facts here. He hasn't been here once since you came in here. That makes him worse than a bum!

TERRY He's workin'!

POP On a Saturday? What about the last two nights? You tellin' me he works twenty-four hours a day now? I don't think so!

TERRY Come on, Pop—

POP —When your wife has a baby you're suppose to be there with her! (TERRY *begins to interrupt, mumbles to herself, etc. . . . as* POP *continues.*) I was always there! Wasn't I? With everyone a youse I was there! I was there with Billy and then Darlene. And I was there when Patrick came along and that pain-in-the-ass brother of yours, Bobby. I was even there all those years later when you showed up. We both thought we were done with all that by then. Hell, I was almost an old man! Your mother was too old to be havin' another. But I was there, wasn't I? When she almost died havin' you? And do you know why?

TERRY I don't care.

POP Because I'm a man! That's why! And that's what men do!

TERRY I know!

POP It's a disgrace! A disgrace, do you hear me?!

TERRY The whole floor can hear you!

POP You're suppose to check out this mornin'?

TERRY Yeah. I told you. So why don't you—

POP —So who's gonna take you home?

TERRY Who do ya think? Chili will be here. He'll be here any minute.

POP Who you think you're kiddin'?

TERRY He's gonna pick me up!

POP Well, what if he doesn't?

TERRY He will! *(Short pause.)* And Yvonne's on her way, too.

POP See?

TERRY We're all goin' to the mother's house. There's gonna be a big party or somethin'. I don't know.

POP And what does the family have to say about all of this? Huh?

TERRY What are they gonna say?

POP Why haven't they pulled him in here to see you?

TERRY *(Softly)* No one knows where he is.

POP Speak up, Terry, when I'm talkin' to ya, please.

TERRY I didn't say nothin'.

POP Well, since he's not here—which by the way your mother predicted would be the case—*(Reaching into his breast pocket)* I got another note from her here.

TERRY Don't you dare read it to me!

POP She made me promise I'd read it to you if that bum of a husband of yours was still missin'.

TERRY When are you gonna stop with this? It's been six months!

POP I'm gonna need my glasses again. *(Pulling his glasses out of his breast pocket, he reads the letter for the first time. He is not a good reader.)* I can't see a thing without 'em these days. Okay, here we go. It starts off, "To my disgrace of a daughter'—

TERRY —Oh my God! Put it away! Burn it.

POP I gotta read it. She made me promise.

TERRY Read it to yourself.

POP I can't. If I tell her I read it to you and I don't, she'll know I'm lyin'.

TERRY How's she gonna know?

POP She knows! Don't ask me how, but she does. How'd she know you were pregnant before you said anythin'? Or that this bum was no good? Huh? She's got a sick sense or somethin'. I'm tellin' ya, between the two of youse you're both makin' me nuts. *(Back to reading)* . . . Okay, disgraceful daughter—"Who woulda thought that I'd end up being the most unhappy mother to walk the face of the planet—"

TERRY All right! Enough!

POP "It's lucky I'm still alive and haven't killed myself by now with the shame you put me through—"

TERRY Give that to me!

POP I gotta read it first.

TERRY I'll read it to myself.

POP No, she said you'd say that.

TERRY She's outta her fuckin' mind!

POP Hey! What's the matta with you talkin' like that?

TERRY She's a freakin' psycho and you know it!

POP She's very upset.

TERRY She's been upset for as long as . . . forever! She's not normal. And she makes you do these stupid things!

POP Hey! She's got a point this time. This is no position for a seventeen-year-old to be in.

TERRY So where is she? She hasn't even come to see her own grand-child! I mean, let's forget about her comin' to see me in the hospital—that would be askin' way too much—but her own grandchild! That's what's a disgrace, Pop!

POP What do you expect from her?

TERRY Nothin'! But why all the time you gotta be takin' her
side?

POP That's what you do when you're married! You wouldn't know
that, bein' in the situation you're in. But when you're married
you stand by each other. Through thick and thin. You don't let
nothin' get between you.

TERRY Not even when one of youse is a nut case?

POP Hey! Shut up!

TERRY Fine.

POP You got some goddamn nerve talkin' about your own mother
like that.

TERRY You see what you do? I can't say anythin'! I can't do anythin' without the both of you jumpin' all over me! It's not fair!
It's not right the way you always listen to her like she makes all
the sense in the world and I'm just a stupid kid!

POP Now, don't get yourself all worked up.

TERRY Now you say that? After you read that hate mail to me?
This is the third letter in two days!

POP Well, I guess you get the drift of it. It goes on a little more
the same way, and then it ends, "Signed your Mother." *(He folds
the letter and hands it to* TERRY.*)* You can finish it later.

TERRY And when is someone gonna tell her she doesn't have to
write the word "signed" at the end of each letter? *(She puts the
letter on the nightstand near her.)*

POP That's the way she is. What'ya gonna do. You gotta take it
with a grain a salt. She means well, Terry.

TERRY How could you say that?

POP Because she does. She's in a lotta pain over this. *(Pause.)* You
know, it's snowin' outside. It's pretty bad out there.

TERRY Are you stayin' or are you leavin'? 'Cause if you're stayin',
why don't you sit down. You're makin' me nervous.

POP You're always nervous, Terry. You gotta get a handle on that. And you're too skinny.

TERRY Oh, now you're losin' your mind. First Ma, now you. I'm as big as a horse, Pop.

POP I didn't think there was even a baby inside you as skinny as you were.

TERRY Oh God. *(Beat.)* Pop, you know I'm gonna have to get ready to leave soon. You wanna go see the baby one more time?

POP Yeah, I could go take a peek.

TERRY Yeah, that's a good idea. 'Cause I have to get dressed and all.

POP So, Yvonne's pickin' you up?

TERRY I said she's comin'.

POP She knows her brother hasn't been around since you got here?

TERRY She knows.

POP And what does she have to say about that?

TERRY Nothin'! I told you. He's workin'!

POP I bet she has nothin' to say. What can you say about a brother who's a bum?

TERRY Enough, Pop. I'll call you in a couple of days, okay?

POP Call me tomorrow. And call me at the plant, I'm gettin' in some overtime these days. Besides, your mother doesn't want you callin' the house.

TERRY No kiddin'! Have I called? Once? Have I?

POP No. You haven't. You've been good about that.

TERRY Go see the baby.

POP I'm gonna do that.

TERRY Good. Okay, then.

POP Biggest mistake of your life.

TERRY Oh, go see the baby, would ya.

POP I'm your father, you know that.

TERRY *(Short pause.)* Yeah? And?

POP *(Beat.)* You need me to talk to the nurses for you?

TERRY For what?

POP Whatever! You need anythin'? You need them to get you anythin'?

TERRY No. Stay away from the nurses, Pop. I mean it.

POP Fine. Bundle up when you leave. *(Beat.)* Okay, I'm gonna go now. I'll talk to you tomorrow, sweetheart. *(He leans over and kisses her on the top of her head.)*

TERRY Bye, Pop.

(POP turns to exit and then spins around.)

POP And make sure they put you in one of those wheelchairs when you're leavin'. You don't wanna break your neck tryin' to leave this place. That's all we'd need.

TERRY Yeah yeah.

(POP exits. TERRY bites her nails, then pulls out the legal-sized papers she hid in the magazine. As she reads she fishes for a pen from her purse. She frets over signing the papers when YVONNE enters. She is wearing a heavy overcoat and boots. Her hat and gloves are in one hand, a shopping bag in the other.)

YVONNE Hey, Mami!

TERRY God, you scared the shit outta me. *(TERRY frantically shoves the papers into the nightstand drawer.)*

YVONNE Let's start partying. What'ya doin'?

TERRY Nothin'. Girl, I'm so glad you're here, you have no idea.

YVONNE Yeah? *(Beat.)* I just saw her again. *Que linda, Mami.* She's just sleepin' like a little angel.

TERRY Sure she's sleepin' now. She was wailin' like crazy the entire time I was tryin' to feed her this mornin'.

YVONNE She ate though, didn't she?

TERRY Oh sure. I'm sore as hell.

YVONNE You're not even dressed. Here, I brought you somethin'. Put it on and let's get outta here!

TERRY What you do this for? Shit, Yvonne, you shouldn't have got me anythin'.

YVONNE Shut up and open it.

(TERRY pulls a cardigan sweater out of the box.)

TERRY Oh my God! It's beautiful!

YVONNE You like it?

TERRY Yeah, but this is too nice. It's too expensive.

YVONNE It's cashmere.

TERRY This musta cost a fortune.

YVONNE Oh my God! Put it on! And I finally remembered your makeup bag like you asked.

TERRY Is my lipstick in it?

YVONNE Yeah, I scoped it out.

TERRY See? It's 'cause I didn't have any makeup that Chili hasn't come to see me yet. Lucky for me, right?

(TERRY pulls off her robe and puts on the sweater that YVONNE brought her. YVONNE tries not to look at her in her bra for too long.)

YVONNE Right. There's three feet a snow on the ground. Have you looked outside?

TERRY *(Continuing to put her sweater on)* No.

YVONNE It's a real mess. *(Turning back to TERRY)* You look beautiful in that.

TERRY I shoulda washed my hair this mornin'.

YVONNE I'll fix it for you. Pants! You need to put pants on!

TERRY My jeans don't fit. I gotta wear my maternity pants. Fuck! I don't want anyone to see me like this.

YVONNE What'ya talkin' about? Mami's cooking and all my aunts and uncles are comin' over. You'll finally meet my cousin. The one I told you about, who's into Santeria and all? She's a trip. She'll tell you your future.

TERRY Yeah, like I wanna hear it.

YVONNE Yeah. Anyway, get dressed.

TERRY It's really cold out, huh?

YVONNE I said! The snow's up to my knees. I don't know if we can even get a cab.

TERRY It's only seven blocks to your mother's.

YVONNE With a baby? What'ya outta your mind?

TERRY No, Yvonne, are you?

YVONNE I'll call José's car service!

TERRY Yeah, okay. Or *(Short pause.)* you could go ahead and I could wait here—

YVONNE What for?

TERRY No, I'm just thinkin' I could wait here for Chili. You know. When he comes—

YVONNE —Yeah, right, just leave this all up to me, okay? You're still a little out of it.

TERRY 'Cause they're all drivin' me crazy here! The nuns, the doctors, those freakin' social workers, or whatever they are! Think they're so superior—

YVONNE —So they ain't nobody.

TERRY They act like they got a right to make me feel . . . cheap or somethin'. I'm tellin' you, it's embarrassin'.

YVONNE Frig 'em. After today you don't need to see any of 'em.

TERRY Afta today, I'm not settin' foot in this place. I don't care if I'm dyin' on the street!

YVONNE So, your Moms come by yet?

TERRY *Paleeezz!* My mother?

YVONNE I don't know . . .

TERRY Forget about it. *(Beat.)* I got another nasty-gram from her today already. You believe that?

YVONNE So she's still wacked-out, huh?

TERRY You kiddin? I'm afraid to walk down the streets alone. I feel like she's gonna jump me from every doorway.

YVONNE Well, what about *(Gestures toward the door)*—what's her name, Terry?

TERRY May.

YVONNE Not your mother! The baby! You gotta name her!

TERRY I don't know yet! Okay? I don't like any of them now!

YVONNE Damn! *(Short pause.)* Name her Yvonne, then.

TERRY Yvonne. Gee, that's such a nice name, Yvonne. I'm gonna wait for Chili.

YVONNE Yeah, by the time he shows up she'll be thirty. *(*TERRY *reacts.)* . . . Sorry.

TERRY He's freakin' out right now! This is a hard time for him.

YVONNE He's goin' through a fuckin' hard time? Girl, what's this fantasy about?

TERRY I can't give up on him now. He's having a reaction is all.

YVONNE Well, when I see him I'm gonna have a reaction all over his face. *Carajo!*

TERRY Maybe he's hurt.

YVONNE Oh, he's gonna be hurtin' all right.

TERRY God, what if he's dead?

YVONNE I hope for his sake he is.

TERRY Could you be serious?

YVONNE You think I'm not serious here?

TERRY Well, I'm worried about him.

YVONNE I can tell you one thing: he's not dead and he's not hurt! He's probably hangin' over at Malavé's. I bet you my mother's left eye. I know I'm right.

TERRY I hope so.

YVONNE You ready to leave soon? Please say yes.

TERRY I have to wait for them to tell me to go. I gotta get signed out, check out or somethin'.

YVONNE So when's that gonna be? (TERRY *shrugs, beat.*) Can I dress her when they bring her in?

TERRY Yeah, okay.

YVONNE Cool. I know! How about if you give her a Spanish name?

TERRY I need somethin' I can pronounce. Poor kid goin' through life and her own mother can't even say her name right. (*Beat.*) Shit, I'm her mother.

YVONNE Man, from now on I'll be Titi Yvonne.

TERRY (*Pause.*) You really think he's at Malavé's? Not with another girl?

YVONNE When I'm right, I'm right. This has Malavé written all over it. Don't worry, I got Luis out there lookin' for him.

TERRY Louie? Yvonne?!

YVONNE What? He's combin' the neighborhood.

TERRY No offense, but he can't even comb his own hair.

YVONNE *Bendito*, how could you talk about Louie like that?

TERRY Don't get me wrong! I love Louie like my own. But he's not exactly the brightest. Am I right or what?

YVONNE *Povricito* Louie. He wanted to help.

TERRY Of all the brothers . . . how did I end up with the one who wouldn't show up for—(*Pause.*) You think he still loves me?

YVONNE Aye, who cares.

TERRY Yvonne!

YVONNE Yes. Of course. Listen, he'll end up comin' back home tonight and you'll have two babies on your hands.

TERRY I just know he's seein' other girls. You know he is, too, don't you? (*Silence.*) You're not answerin' me.

YVONNE What do I know? *(Referring to* TERRY's *makeup)* Let me see what you're doin' there.

TERRY What can you do? You can't do nothin' to this.

YVONNE I'll put it back. It'll look nice.

TERRY No, it won't.

YVONNE Give me your brush. Man, what a fuckin' baby. *(*YVONNE *sits on the bed with* TERRY *and brushes her hair.)* What's the matta with you? *(Referring to her hair)* Hold still now. Mira, there. You look great.

TERRY Oh yeah, sure, you can't tell me I don't look like a fuckin' truck.

YVONNE You look like a fuckin' nut, is what you look like!

TERRY Maybe I am goin' nuts.

YVONNE God, what now?

TERRY You think I'm kiddin', right? You got no idea. *(*TERRY *pulls a cigarette out of her purse and brings it to her mouth.* YVONNE *slaps it out of her hand.)* I could just walk out right now like nothin' happened, you know?

YVONNE Oh, you are buggin' me out.

TERRY No, like I was just visitin' someone. Just another person. Weird, right? What could they do? How would they even know? I'm tellin' ya, my mind's thinkin' all sorts of strange things right now. Not that I'd do it or anythin', but . . .

YVONNE That's it! What do you have to do? Tell them you're ready or somethin'?

TERRY I don't know. Maybe they'll just tell me when I have to leave.

YVONNE So should I go and find a nurse?

TERRY For what?

YVONNE *(Heading for the door.)* So we can get the hell outta here!

ENSEMBLE STUDIO THEATRE MARATHON 2000

TERRY No, you don't have to do that! They don't like it when you talk to them!

(YVONNE *moves to the door and opens it. She leans out into the hall and . . .*)

YVONNE What are you doin'?

LUIS (*Offstage*) What?

YVONNE What are you doin' standin' out here like that?

LUIS I was lookin' for the room number: 406.

YVONNE You found it. Get in here.

(LUIS *enters the room.* YVONNE *follows him and lets the door close behind them.* LUIS *is wearing an oversized overcoat and a woolen cap pulled down to his eyes.*)

LUIS Was'up, was'up, Terry! You a moms now! Much props to you, dude. This must be a very exciting time for ya. Yeah, like havin' a baby and shit. Very choice. Very choice. We're all proud. Congratulations and . . . yeah. (*To* YVONNE) I been lookin' all over for Chili, man, I can't find him nowhere. Can I stop now? It's like snowin' out there.

TERRY Sure you can.

LUIS Hey, check this out! They got a room down there loaded with little babies in these little carts all lined up and shit. It looks like a little baby army. Word! And some of them little dudes are in blue—bet that's 'cause they're boys and some of 'em are in little pink caps—'cause that would make 'em girls. You gotta see this! (*Beat.*) Where's your little baby, Terry?

TERRY She's in the nursery.

LUIS The baby room? I didn't recognize her. Which one was she?

YVONNE What'ya mean you've been lookin' everywhere? You've only been at it for (*Checking her watch*) like twenty minutes.

LUIS I can't find him. I'm bein' square with ya, man. He's like nowhere to be found. It's freaky, dude.

YVONNE Where'd you look?

LUIS Huh?

YVONNE Where'd you go lookin' for him?

LUIS Where he likes to go, man. I went to the park—you know? Near the swings and the fountain with the fake animals—those big bunnies and that bad-ass bear.

YVONNE Louie, that's where you like to go. I told ya ya had to go to his friends' houses to see if he was with any of them.

LUIS Oh, I did! I did!

YVONNE *(Skeptical)* You did?

LUIS Yeah, little sis! Sure I did.

YVONNE Well?

LUIS He wasn't there either!

TERRY I told you, Yvonne, this is too much for him.

YVONNE Whose house did you go to?

LUIS That dude with the bike? You know who I'm talkin' about?

YVONNE Who?

TERRY Benny. He's talkin' about Benny Bug Eyes.

LUIS Yeah, he wasn't there. I don't know where Chili's gone, man. *(To* YVONNE*)* Ya got any idea where he might be?

YVONNE If I knew, would I have had you out there in the snow lookin' for him?

LUIS Whoa! This must be a trip for you, Terry, huh? You bein' married to him and all. Very heavy from your point of view. Ya like worried?

YVONNE No, she's not worried.

TERRY Louie, when was the last time you saw him?

LUIS The last time?

TERRY Yeah.

YVONNE *(Losing her patience)* The last time you saw him, when was it?!

LUIS Hey, let's go see the baby. Can I go see the baby in that baby room?

TERRY In a little while. This is important, Louie. Please try to remember.

LUIS Oh, I can remember good, man. I got a excellent memory G.

TERRY So when was it?

(Silence.)

YVONNE Now you gotta repeat the question.

TERRY Louie, when was the last time you saw Chili?

LUIS This mornin', eating breakfast.

YVONNE What?

LUIS Yeah, eating Wheat Chex, dude. He wanted some Product 19 but—we didn't have any. I told ya, my memory is very good.

TERRY Yvonne?!

YVONNE I was waitin' for him at your place! I haven't been home since last night.

TERRY So, so then your mother knows. Why didn't she call me?

YVONNE *(To* LUIS*)* Where was Mami? Was she there, too?

LUIS Nah, just me and Chili. He told me to not say nothin' about him eatin' Wheat Chex and shit. Said he'd kick my ass—he said that. Like he could do that! Know what I'm sayin'? He can't kick my ass, man, I can kick his ass! You ask anybody. Ask Jimmy, he'll—

TERRY *(To* YVONNE, *interrupting* LUIS*)* He's left me!

YVONNE You don't know that for sure.

TERRY Sure I do. He's eating cereal over at your house this mornin' like nothin's happened. And I know he hasn't come to see me. I'm pretty damn clear on that!

YVONNE *(To* LUIS*)* What did the *pendejo* look like? What did he say?

LUIS He looked like Chili, Yvonne. That was him, man. I know my little bro when I see him. When can we see the little baby room? That was mad funny! All them lined up like that.

TERRY Did he seem upset?

LUIS *(Realizing he's being spoken to)* Who me?

TERRY Yeah, Louie, did he seem nervous or angry or somethin'?

LUIS Who? Chili? Nah! He was chill. He was serious hungry, though. He ate like two bowls of the stuff. And then he wanted me to make him toast, but I don't get along with that toaster no more.

TERRY Did he say anythin' about me?

LUIS About you, Terry? Uhm, let me think. Nope. I don't think so, man. He didn't say . . . Nope. He didn't say nothin' about you. He talked about Papi a little.

YVONNE *(To LUIS)* Give it a rest already, would ya? For Christsake!

LUIS What you so upset about, dude?

YVONNE Shut up, let me think.

TERRY What's there to think about?

YVONNE Listen, whatever happens, it's gonna be okay.

TERRY Are you kiddin'? Nothin's okay here. Everythin's shit now. I kept thinkin' he'd walk through that door any minute. With flowers and "I'm sorry, babe" and "I was workin' real hard to get us more money for the baby" and I don't think I can do this anymore. I can't do this!

YVONNE He'll come to his senses. He can't just walk out on you like that. He's an idiot, but he's not that stupid.

LUIS Nah, Chili's not stupid, man.

(POP storms into the room, headed directly toward LUIS.)

POP I knew I'd find you, you son-of-a-bitch!

LUIS Yo, yo! Was'up with this shit?

TERRY Pop!! That's not Chili!

POP I'm gonna kill you for what you did to my daughter!

TERRY That's Louie, his brother!

(POP *stops dead in his tracks.*)

POP You're kiddin' me, right?

LUIS I ain't no fighter! Best to step away, man.

YVONNE That's my brother Luis, Mr. D.

POP No!

LUIS Dude! You must be Terry's old man!

POP He looks just like the other one!

TERRY No, he doesn't! Chili's good-lookin'.

LUIS Yeah, Chili's most handsome. I have to give him that.

POP What's the matta with him? He retarded?

YVONNE Mr. D., I gotta ask you not to talk like that about my brother.

LUIS Oh! Snap! She dissed you good!

POP *(To* TERRY*)* Is this young man high? You got a drug addict in your hospital room?

TERRY No! What are you—

LUIS —Nah, nah, that's okay, Terry. Nah, Mr. Dude, a lot a people think I'm a druggie—that's no problem. Let me explain. *(Beat.)* First, it's the way I dress—

POP Get him outta here!

TERRY Try to be nice! He's been out lookin' for Chili.

POP Yeah?

TERRY Yeah.

POP *(To* LUIS*)* So where is your brother the bum?

LUIS It's a mystery, man. It's like he's disappeared off the face of the planet. Word!

POP *(To* TERRY*)* Another useless wonder.

TERRY Yvonne, why don't you take Louie to see the baby.

YVONNE Can we please go soon? I'll call José for the car. *(*TERRY *nods. To* LUIS*)* Come on. Let's go see your niece.

LUIS Whoa! Check this out! Oh, man! I'm a uncle and shit!

POP *(To* TERRY*)* Listen to that language!

LUIS *(To* POP*)* Much props to ya, Mr. Dude. *(He holds up his hand to* POP, *who ignores him.)* I'll see ya when I see ya. So *(Beat.)* Terry—with all my extreme sincerity of emotion, I wanna say . . . congratulations for makin' me a uncle!

TERRY Thanks for comin' by. I'll see you at the house in a little while.

LUIS Definitely! Peace out!

YVONNE I'll be right back.

*(*YVONNE *and* LUIS *exit.)*

TERRY *(Pause.)* I thought you were goin' home.

POP I thought I was, too. My plans kinda changed.

TERRY *(Pause.)* This isn't lookin' too good, Pop.

POP I know.

TERRY I didn't think it would turn out this way.

POP What do you know. You're too young to figure the way things are gonna turn out. It's not your fault.

TERRY You don't think so?

POP I don't. *(Beat.)* No, I don't.

TERRY But Ma does.

POP Yeah, I suppose she does.

TERRY Pop? Can I ask you somethin'?

POP What'ya wanna know?

TERRY You think Ma would let me move back home?

POP *(Pause, then slowly)* You know, when I left before, I was all ready, with my coat all buttoned and my hat on, and I was preparin' to hit that cold wind in my face. And there—as I got to the double doors downstairs—was your mother. *(*TERRY *opens her mouth to speak.* POP *continues.)* She was standin' there between the revolvin' doors and the doors that let you into the buildin'.

Not outside and not inside either. She was just there between the two. When I saw her standin' there, I said to myself, Well, she's finally come to her senses and sees how much you need her now. How much she really needs you, too, if she would think about it for a minute, and I felt so good inside. For that minute I was thankin' God for bringin' my wife back to me. For bringin' your mother back to you and—then I saw it in her hand and I knew it wasn't any different. She got herself as close as she could and she couldn't get any closer than she was. (POP *takes out a letter from his coat pocket.*) She said to me that if I didn't deliver this to you now that she would never talk to me again. (TERRY *starts to cry.*) I don't think I could go through that, Terry. The way you have? I don't think I could take it. So here I am. Your father. And her husband. And I can't help either one of ya. She asked me to read this one all the way through this time 'cause she knows I haven't read any of 'em all the way through yet. She knows me, Terry.

TERRY (*Breaking down*) Why are you doing this to me?

POP Terry. Let me do this now and get it over with. (*He pulls his glasses out of his pocket.*)

TERRY No! No! Get outta here!

POP But you don't understand—

TERRY —I can't! I can't take another! Why? Why do you wanna—

POP —I'm just tryin' to keep you and your mother together.

TERRY Stop tryin' so hard! You're fuckin' killin' me!

POP She's got a right to say what she feels!

TERRY Yvonne!

POP But this is the only way she can talk to you right now. Don't you get it? She's tryin' to keep in touch this way. Just let me read it, okay? Let me try to make her happy.

TERRY Yvonne!

POP Stop it. You're actin' crazy! It's one lousy note, Terry. You're a big girl now. Let your mother have her say. What's one more, right? *(TERRY covers her ears with her hands.)* "To my blah, blah . . ." We know how that goes, don't we? "How could you take this evil into your life? I have scheduled an exorcism for you without your father's knowledge as he seems to be in collusion with you and your Puerto Rican family."

(YVONNE runs into the room.)

YVONNE What happened?! What's the matta?!

TERRY Tell him to go!

POP All I'm doin' is—Okay, I won't read it.

TERRY Get outta here!!

POP What am I gonna say to her? I can't go down there and tell her I didn't read this to you.

TERRY Give it to me! Give it! *(She grabs the letter out of POP's hand.)* I got it, all right? You tell her I got her goddamn fuckin' letter!

POP You shouldn't—

TERRY —Go to her! She's waitin' for you. So go on, you love her so much!

POP What the hell's the matta with you?! She's my wife!

TERRY Oh God!

POP How you gonna treat me like this? Who's been the one with you through this whole thing?

TERRY *(To YVONNE)* He doesn't get it! Oh my God, he doesn't get it! *(To POP)* You think you're helpin' me here or somethin'?

YVONNE Calm down, Terry.

TERRY *(To YVONNE)* Don't you dare start! Don't.

(YVONNE throws up her hands.)

POP Theresa—

TERRY No, no, no, no—you can't talk to me anymore! Just go. Do me that favor, Pop, or my head's gonna explode!

POP *(To* YVONNE*)* You talk to her!

YVONNE You can't be serious!

TERRY I said get the hell outta here!

POP If I leave now, that's it. I'm not gonna put myself through this with you anymore. Is that what you want? *(Pause.)* I'm the one who's kept this family together, you know! Me! Back and forth. Every day listenin' to the yellin' on one side and the cryin' on the other. What'ya want from me? *(Silence.)* You can't talk to me like that you know. I'm your father.

TERRY Bye, Pop.

*(*POP *heads for the door.)*

POP Aren't you tired of making mistake afta mistake? *(He exits.)*

YVONNE *(Pause.)* I called José for the cab. He's on his way. *(Silence.)* You ready?

TERRY I don't know.

YVONNE Come on, let's get outta here. This whole thing has gotten too freaky. I just wanna go home now.

TERRY He did the right thing, Yvonne.

YVONNE Who?!

TERRY Chili. He's the smartest one of us all.

YVONNE What are you talkin' about?

TERRY He got pushed into all of this. I wanted so much to be a part of your family.

YVONNE It's gonna work out. Mami will let you move in with us. It'll be great, just the two of us.

TERRY I wanted out. Don't you see? I knew I'd get pregnant.

YVONNE Hey! Chili is just as responsible for that as you are!

TERRY I told him he didn't need anythin'. Shit, I did it.

YVONNE So what?!

TERRY It wasn't fair. What I did. It wasn't fair to him. And he married me anyway. Why did I do that?

YVONNE Let's get the baby ready. We're gonna have to wrap her in at least two blankets.

TERRY He never said what I did. Did he?

YVONNE Terry, it's almost eleven.

TERRY You knew it. I told you. I told you the next day. Remember? They all knew here. They could tell. How could they tell?

YVONNE I put the crib up last night. It's all ready. I wanted to surprise you. I know we said it didn't have to go up for a couple of months, but I figured we could put the bassinet in it.

TERRY They're trained to know about these things. They could tell by lookin' at me that I shouldn't have a baby.

YVONNE Terry, let's go, please. Mami's cookin' lunch.

TERRY No, maybe I should do what the lady said.

YVONNE What lady?

TERRY The social worker, whatever she is. The one who kept comin' in and talkin' to me. *(She picks up the adoption papers she had in her nightstand.)* She said there were a lot of really nice couples with money. Rich people with houses and shit. They can't have their own babies, and it's a shame, 'cause they're the ones who want babies the most.

YVONNE Are you outta your mind?

TERRY They pay you a lot of money. A lot. I could go back to school. Maybe even go to college or somethin'.

YVONNE This is normal. The way you're feelin'? It's normal. It's called postnatal depression. Everyone goes through it. Just wait a few days. It'll go away.

TERRY Maybe there's another room. One with all the mothers that should keep their babies. Maybe that's why I'm alone in here. 'Cause they know I'm no good. They know I should give her to them.

YVONNE Let's go.

TERRY That's why I'm in here. Don't you see? They couldn't talk to me like they did if there was other mothers and babies in here.

YVONNE You're losin' it. Just stop talkin' and get ready. I'm tellin' you this will pass.

TERRY What? What's gonna pass? Me? I'm gonna wake up tomorrow and be someone else? I don't think so! This is me. I'm not gonna pass, Yvonne!

YVONNE You're talkin' like it's the end of the world. She's just a little baby. You have me. You have Mami. We're all gonna help. You're not alone in this.

TERRY I am alone.

YVONNE Stop it! This is ridiculous. Come on. We gotta go.

TERRY That's why she doesn't have a name! I can't even name her!

YVONNE You're not givin' this baby away!

TERRY I have to.

YVONNE No, you don't! Let's go. Right now! I mean it!

TERRY Tell them I wanna talk to them.

YVONNE No!

TERRY Yes! They don't tell you to give up your baby unless you really should.

YVONNE Terry, you're scarin' me! Stop it. This is my niece. I'm not gonna let anythin' bad happen to you or the baby, I promise!

TERRY I can't! I can't keep her!

YVONNE You have to!

TERRY Why? Because you want me to? I don't deserve her. She deserves a lot better than me.

YVONNE Get dressed!

TERRY Call them in.

YVONNE Get dressed, bitch!

TERRY I'll tell them myself. *(She gets out of bed and starts to dress.)*

YVONNE I'm not playin' with you. This baby's goin' with us.

TERRY She's not your baby!

YVONNE Then give her to me!

TERRY What?

YVONNE Yeah. Give her to me, Terry.

TERRY How could you say that?

YVONNE You don't want her? Well, I do.

TERRY No no no. I'm not gonna give her to you. How could you . . . No, don't say that! *(Breaking down)* She's my baby!!

YVONNE *(Breaking down)* Of course she is!! That's all I'm sayin'! She's your baby. Isn't she?

TERRY Yeah. *(Beat.)* But—

YVONNE —You can do it, Terry.

TERRY I'm scared!

YVONNE I'll never leave you!

TERRY You . . . you promise?

YVONNE I swear to God!

TERRY Cross your heart and hope to die?

YVONNE And hope to die.

TERRY *(Short pause.)* I don't know if I can do this.

YVONNE Of course you can.

TERRY What if I can't?

YVONNE You will. You'll see.

TERRY You promise you'll always be with me?

YVONNE I promise I'll never leave you.

TERRY *(Short pause.)* Shit, if my mother can do it. Right?

YVONNE Are you kiddin'? You'll be a thousand times better.

TERRY A thousand times better.

YVONNE Listen, I'm gonna go downstairs and wait for José's car.

TERRY Okay, I'll let them know we're leavin'.

YVONNE What's the matta? Just pick up the phone.

TERRY Yeah, I know.

YVONNE And be sure to bundle the baby up good. I wanted to dress her, but she really should be dressed by her mother.

TERRY I will.

YVONNE I'll see you down there. Hurry, okay?

TERRY Yeah, okay.

(YVONNE *exits.* TERRY *stares at the phone for a few seconds and picks up the receiver, waiting to hear the other side pick up.*)

Hello? Yes, hi, hello—this—is—Teresa Torres? In room— uhm—oh God, I'm not sure what number. It's a semiprivate and I am all alone in it? Uhm, they said I should pick up the— call and tell you when I'm ready to take my baby home? (*Pause.*) Yes. Baby Girl Torres? I mean her name is, her name isn't on her—the wristband—it says Baby Girl Torres, but it's gonna be . . . her name . . . her name . . . it's gonna be . . . it's gonna be . . . her name is Maggie. (*Pause, getting a little embarrassed*) Yes! Right, okay. (*Starts to break down*) So, I'll just wait here? Yeah. Yes. Okay. Thank you. (*She hangs up the phone and tries desperately not to cry as she inhales deeply.*) . . . Maggie.

(*Closing music begins to play.*)

(*Lights fade to black.*)

Cannibals

2000 >HEATHER DUNDAS

ORIGINAL EST PRODUCTION

DIRECTOR India Cooper

SET DESIGNER Carlo Adinolfi

COSTUME DESIGNER Bruce Goodrich

SOUND Robert Gould

PROPS Laura Raynor

PRODUCTION STAGE MANAGER Jim Ring

STAGE MANAGER Courtney Todd Stuart

The cast was as follows:

JANE Diana LaMar

SIERRA Miranda Black

MAX Lou Carbonneau

PERSEPHONE Annie Meisels

RACHEL Anna Antonia Li

Cannibals was originally part of a series of one-act plays by Heather Dundas called *Ghost Stories*. It was presented at Glaxa Studios in Los Angeles by The Wilton Project. (Director, Charlie Stratton. Featuring Tim Choate, Alexandra Hedison, O-Lan Jones, Deirdre O'Connell, and Sandra Purpuro.)

CHARACTERS

(Note: All children's parts must be played by adult actors.)

JANE thirty-five, she has a Band-Aid on her nose

SIERRA seven, Jane's daughter, she is confident

MAX three, Jane's son

PERSEPHONE seven, a girl in Sierra's first-grade class; she is very
  high-strung

RACHEL seven, another girl in Sierra's class, a sad sack

PLACE

Jane's car

TIME

Monday, 7:50 a.m.

Lights up on JANE, SIERRA, PERSEPHONE, *and* MAX. *They are in a car.*

MAX *(Looking out the window)* Car. Car. Red car. Truck.

SIERRA *(To* PERSEPHONE*)* This morning? Well, you know how my
  mom has a really bad temper sometimes?

PERSEPHONE Yeah?

MAX *Big* truck. Car. Car.

SIERRA This morning she made Max cry.

JANE Sierra, I didn't mean to—

MAX Truck! Look, Mommy! Red truck! It's—*firetruck!!!!*

(They all watch in silence as the truck goes by.)

JANE Look at that. Wow, Max.

SIERRA He loves firetrucks.

PERSEPHONE I *know*, Sierra.

SIERRA I'm just *telling* you!

PERSEPHONE Well, *duh*.

SIERRA I just thought since you don't *have* a brother, since *your* parents are divorced—

JANE Sier-*ra*!

PERSEPHONE Yesterday night my mom's friend took me to the library, because you know I'm really interested in cannibals?

SIERRA I didn't mean to give you a putdown about your bad temper, Mommy.

JANE 'S ckay. Rachel's house. *(She pulls into a driveway. She unlocks and opens the passenger door.)*

PERSEPHONE And there's this one tribe? And they used to *eat brains*.

SIERRA Brains of other people?

PERSEPHONE Yes.

SIERRA Raw?

PERSEPHONE Yes. Completely raw.

SIERRA What did they taste like?

PERSEPHONE Eeeuw. I don't know. *Disgusting*.

SIERRA Like thoughts, maybe. Like whatever the person was thinking when the cannibal got him—

PERSEPHONE But not for food. They didn't eat brains for food.

SIERRA Then why—?

JANE Oh, for Pete's sake, where is she?

(JANE honks the horn. MAX immediately claps his hands over his ears.)

MAX *Quiet!!!*

JANE I have an 8:30 deposition! *(She honks again.)*

MAX Mommy, don't make noise!

SIERRA *(Simultaneously)* Mommy, why did cannibals—

JANE Sierra, go ring the bell for Rachel.

SIERRA But, Mommy, why—

JANE Go on! Hurry up!

MAX *Quiet, Mommy!*

JANE *Hush*, Max!

(SIERRA *runs off.*)

JANE Max, I can talk if I want to.

MAX I want you to be quiet!

JANE But, Max, I'm the mommy, that means I'm the boss—

PERSEPHONE Jane?

JANE —that means I *can* talk if I want to!

(MAX *starts to cry.*)

MAX Don't yell at me.

PERSEPHONE Jane?

JANE I'm not yelling at you! Don't cry!

PERSEPHONE Jane?

MAX *(Sniffling) Scary* Mommy.

JANE Aw, Max—

PERSEPHONE Jane?

JANE *Yes*, Persephone?!

PERSEPHONE Why do cannibals eat brains?

JANE Um. I don't know.

PERSEPHONE But why do you *think*?

JANE . . . Because everyone they know does it.

PERSEPHONE And they don't want to be left out?

JANE Guess not. Good morning, Rachel!

(SIERRA *enters, followed by* RACHEL, *who is clumsily carrying a lunchbox, library books, a teddy bear, some papers, and a raincoat.*)

RACHEL My housekeeper couldn't find my library books. It's kinda hard when that happens.

JANE Get in the car, please. We're late.

(RACHEL *doesn't move.*)

RACHEL This morning, my cat? You know my cat, Sierra?

Remember my cat? Marmalade? Well, she was over there by that bush? See the bush over there? That's where she was. *(She starts to indicate the bush and drops her library books and papers. She looks at the papers impassively.)* Oh, gosh. My papers fell. They're all over.

JANE *(Tightly)* Pick. Them. Up.

(RACHEL doesn't move.)

RACHEL Oh, there's a lot of them. It's kinda hard when you drop your papers and no one helps you and there's a lot of them—

JANE *Pick them up! Now!*

RACHEL Oh, gosh. *(She ineptly starts to pick up the papers, one at a time.)*

SIERRA See, it's just my mom's bad temper, like I said.

(Lights shift.)

SIERRA Like this morning. Max didn't want to put on his shoes.

MAX *(Overlapping)* I said no shoes! No shoes for Max!

PERSEPHONE She said:

RACHEL, MAX, PERSEPHONE, AND SIERRA PUT ON YOUR SHOES!

SIERRA Bang! Crying. He always cries.

JANE I didn't want to make him cry! All I wanted to do was put his shoes on so we could get to the damn school on time! *He just wouldn't listen to me!*

(Lights shift again. JANE is released from the reality of the car and can wander freely about the stage. The children continue in the reality of the car. RACHEL continues to pick the papers up, one by one. When she's finished, she sits down in her chair. MAX looks out the window. SIERRA plays with her hair. As JANE prowls around, they are oblivious to her. As far as they are concerned, JANE is still driving the car.)

JANE I just don't get it! The simplest thing. Put on your shoes. No! he screams as though I'm going to cut his toes off! *No shoes!* Then he runs to the other side of the room. Come here, I say, trying to keep my voice steady, come here and put your shoes on. *No!!* he screams, *no shoes!!* And I think, Well, who cares anyway about shoes. So I'm going to drop the whole thing, except then he sees me slowing down for a second so he grabs the shoes and throws them at me, and one of them smacks me in the face. Right on the bridge of my nose. So hard it makes my eyes water.

Okay. So now it's one of those slowly-I-turn moments. I pick the little red Keds up from the floor and I'm chasing him and I'm going to grab him and jam the shoes on his horrible little feet no matter *how loud* he screams, and he's wailing, and I realize I've assumed this panting, raisin-eyed, apelike stance and I think, *What am I doing?*

I drop the shoes, slam the bedroom door, and go find the Marlboros I have hidden in the back of my closet. *(She shakily lights a cigarette and stands downstage smoking it.)*

Here's what I don't understand. Ten years ago I was a bisexual in New Orleans. I was clerking at a law firm, I had a set of intimidating suits and one really effective fuck-me outfit, and I cared deeply about the U.S. presence in El Salvador. Then I met a man, a very nice man, and we talked about art and commitment and politics, and the sex was fantastic, and then, sort of as a ploy for a party, and sort of as a way to save on rent, we got married, and before I know it and despite my best efforts I'm pregnant, and the thought of aborting a fetus with this man's DNA—even though I support the right in general—is too awful to think of, and so I go ahead and have it, and seven years after that here I am. And I drive in a *carpool* for Christsake, and I scream at a three-year-old about his *sneakers* and I wonder, Is this really the life I chose?

Because I'm not good at this. And I think I need to get out of it.

(SIERRA *and* PERSEPHONE *simultaneously see something outside the window.*)

SIERRA AND PERSEPHONE *Punchbug!*

(SIERRA *punches* MAX *on the arm while* PERSEPHONE *punches* RACHEL *on the arm.*)

SIERRA AND PERSEPHONE Punchbug can't punch me back!

MAX Where?

RACHEL Ow!

SIERRA Over there! A blue one!

RACHEL You hurt my arm!

PERSEPHONE That's the game, duh.

MAX *Where?*

SIERRA *(Pointing)* Over there.

(MAX *looks at a different angle, doesn't see anything.* SIERRA *takes his head and forces him to look the right way.*)

SIERRA *There.*

MAX Oh!

RACHEL *I really hate it when you hurt my arm!*

MAX Punchbug Can't punch me back! (*He tries to punch* SIERRA, *but she dodges out of the way.*)

SIERRA You can't punch me!

PERSEPHONE *(To* RACHEL*)* Grow *up*, Rachel.

MAX *Yes!* I *saw* the blue car!

SIERRA *No!* I said *can't* punch me back!

MAX *Yes!*

SIERRA *No!*

(MAX *swings again at* SIERRA. *She dodges again, laughing. He swings again and again, getting more frustrated and upset each time. She continues to dodge away.*)

MAX Stay still so I can hit you!

RACHEL *It's really terrible when you hurt me!*

(RACHEL *lunges at* PERSEPHONE, *grabbing her by the neck.* PERSEPHONE *shrieks.* JANE *does not have to literally return to the car, however, there should be a light shift or some other indication that she is now tuning into the children.*)

JANE Stop it!

(MAX *covers his ears and quakes.*)

PERSEPHONE But she grabbed my *neck*!

RACHEL She hit me first!

SIERRA I *said* can't punch me back!

JANE I don't care.

PERSEPHONE But—

JANE *I don't care! (Pause.)* Now. If I hear one more person *yelling* I'm going to *stop the car* and you can all *walk* to school. Understand?

SIERRA *(Sorry)* Yes.

MAX *(Sniffling)* Yes, Mama.

(Pause.)

JANE Persephone? Rachel?

PERSEPHONE . . . You can't do that.

JANE Why not?

PERSEPHONE It's a threat, and it's not okay to use threats on children.

JANE It's worse if I drive the car into a wall, like I might if you all don't shut up, Persephone . . .

PERSEPHONE Hey, my mom's a *lawyer*—

JANE *I'm* a lawyer—

PERSEPHONE But you're on the mommy track and my mom's a partner—

(JANE'*s off again on a tangent.*)

JANE To my husband, people will say, "Hi, how's work?" and then they'll talk about a particular case for a while. To me, people say,

"Hi, how're the *kids?*" with this really sappy little smirk on their faces.

RACHEL My dad's a *judge* . . . He could send your mom to jail, Persephone.

JANE Just once, I'd like to look into someone's dishonest, patronizing, sentimental face—"How're the *kids?*"—and tell them the truth. That I walked into the adorable little-girl tea party in my kitchen last week, and there they were—

*(*SIERRA, PERSEPHONE, *and* RACHEL *click imaginary teacups.)*

SIERRA, PERSEPHONE, AND RACHEL A toast to Satan!

JANE —but of course no one would believe me. I've also secretly always wanted to answer the question:

(The children stand and shout.)

SIERRA, PERSEPHONE, RACHEL, AND MAX Hi! How're the kids?

JANE *(answering them)* "Oh . . . didn't you hear about the . . . tragedy?" *(Children sit back down, resume reality of the car.)*—but of course I won't, because I'm positive saying that would call down some huge karmic jinx on one if not both of my children. I mean, I don't believe in jinxes or ghosts or angels or any of that paranormal shit, but still. *(She finds herself back in the car, driving.)*

RACHEL I've seen a ghost.

JANE You have?

SIERRA Wow.

MAX Ghosts are scary.

RACHEL My ghost isn't scary. She's a little girl and she comes into my room at night sometimes.

JANE At night? Maybe you're asleep and dreaming that you saw a ghost . . .

RACHEL Oh no. She's real. I know she's real.

SIERRA What does she look like?

RACHEL She's green.

PERSEPHONE Green?

RACHEL *All* green, kind of like a computer screen.

JANE Rachel, have you ever told your mom about what you think you're seeing?

RACHEL My mom sees her, too. She introduced us.

JANE Uh-huh.

(JANE *starts pacing around, as though she were pushing a shopping cart. The children get out greasepaint crayons and start to draw on each other's faces.* SIERRA *is a princess,* PERSEPHONE *is a witch,* RACHEL *is a cat,* MAX *is a dog.*)

JANE I like to walk through Kmart. I just cruise the aisles slowly, putting plastic stuff in my cart. It relaxes me. And no matter how much I put in the cart, it only comes to $100 or so. It's great.

And I'm buying things like . . . kids' socks. I'm obsessing about getting the *right* shade of, say, blue in the sock. And I'm worrying whether it's 100 percent cotton or only 85 percent, in which case am I paying too much for it? And then I wonder if some child in El Salvador made that sock, for slave wages, breathing in toxic dust? And then I realize that, if I do in fact find out that the sock is made under inhumane conditions in El Salvador, the only action I can take at this point is not to buy it. This is totally wimpy as far as political action goes, and not at all what I would have done ten years ago. But this is my life now.

There're always lots of other women there, shopping, and I wonder how much they're really looking to buy things they need and how much they're searching to change what they already have? I can tell by how much shopping I'm doing how depressed I'm getting.

What a pathetic life. Maybe I should drive into a wall.

(The children are still drawing on each other's faces. JANE *stands off to one side and watches them dispassionately.)*

SIERRA *(Suggesting a game)* Pretend we're slaves?

RACHEL Yeah, we're slaves and we're really poor.

PERSEPHONE But we *look* good.

SIERRA Yeah, we're really beautiful.

MAX What about me? Am I a slave?

RACHEL No, you're a *boy*.

PERSEPHONE *Boys* can't be slaves.

MAX But I want to—

SIERRA You can be our dog. The dog of the beautiful poor slave girls.

MAX Okay!

*(*MAX *starts barking happily.* JANE *starts walking around and around the children.)*

JANE And the thing is, you go through these days and they seem so monotonous and unimportant, but if you're three, or seven, *nothing's* unimportant. Everything's *vital*. And you never really know what trivial, unimportant little event is going to stick in their minds for some reason and become iconic in their lives.

It's *terrifying*: I am the most important person in my children's lives. Imagine that.

*(*SIERRA *leaves the car and walks over to* JANE.*)*

SIERRA Mama, do you like my picture? *(She hands it to* JANE.*)*

JANE Mmmmm. *Lots* of red and blue . . . very nice.

SIERRA It's Max drowning after he was bitten by a jellyfish.

JANE *(To* SIERRA*)* Ah. *(To herself)* It's *my* face imbedded in their psyches forever, indelibly. They might hate me, they might be embarrassed by me, they might even think they've forgotten me, but I will always, always be there. Should I get off on this? Should I believe twentieth-century psychoanalysis, which tells me that I want to use them as little staging grounds for my own neuroses?

(SIERRA *walks with* JANE, *holding hands.*)

JANE Sierra, are you happy?

SIERRA Most of the time. Sometimes I'm too busy. Sometimes I just have to cry. Sometimes Max drives me crazy. Are you happy?

JANE I . . . of course I am.

SIERRA I'm going to be an artist when I grow up. And a teacher. And a mother. And a lawyer. And an ice skater.

JANE All at the same time?

SIERRA I want to be like you, Mama.

(SIERRA *runs away from* JANE, *resumes her place in the car.* JANE *continues pacing.*)

JANE Like me. Now *there's* a question: What's in this for me? Will I ever see New Orleans again? Will I ever have sex with a woman again? Will I ever have sex again at all? Do I even care? Have I done the right thing by concentrating my focus so directly and specifically on only two small human beings? Is it true that the hand that rocks the cradle rules the world?

SIERRA Let's paint Mama's face, too!

JANE Okay, so it's not all bad. I've learned how to love people who drool when I kiss them. I get hugged good morning with four arms and four legs. I muddle through my mommy-track job and every so often get an amazing insight from my children. I even still love my husband, although we often feel like two oxen at the same yoke. (*She sits back down in the car.*)

JANE (*To* SIERRA) Oh, I— What would you draw on me?

SIERRA A princess.

PERSEPHONE A witch.

RACHEL A slave.

MAX A dog.

JANE *(To herself)* Is this enough for a lifetime? *Is it?* Why do I keep
thinking about driving my car into a wall? *(To the children)* I
don't think I want to get painted—*(They all start to come after her
with their gooky crayons. She tries to push them off, but they keep
trying.* JANE *ends up with several war-paint stripes on her face. One of
the crayons catches her in the eye.)* Ow! Guys, back off now, okay?
*(The children laugh and go after her again, even more excitedly. She
again tries to push them away.)* I mean it! Back off! *(Suddenly
something appears in front of the car.* JANE *swerves the car and stomps
on the brakes. We hear honking. All the children are thrown with the
centripetal force of the swerve. The car screeches to a stop.)* Stop it! I
said stop it! Why don't you *listen* to me?! *(Shaking, she puts her
hands over her face for a moment to collect herself. She turns and looks
at the children to make sure they're okay. They stare back at her,
terrified. With forced calm)* Okay. Just—put the face paints away.
And nobody *touch* me while I'm *driving.*

*(*JANE *resumes driving. Silence for a moment.)*

MAX Car. Car. Car. Jeep. Car. Truck. Truck. Car. Car.

JANE *(In desperation)* Tell us some more about cannibals,
Persephone.

PERSEPHONE So there was this woman? And she went walking?
Through Africa? And she bumped right smack into the
cannibals. And they didn't eat her. I don't know why. I think
she had really fine clothes on. Like those adventure clothes that
have those hard hats, you know? And a white scarf. And a long,
beautiful skirt. But they didn't eat her. Instead, they gave her a
present. And she took the present and put it into her hard
adventure hat and walked back out of the jungle. And when she
got back, she took off her hat and took out her present. And she
opened it. And you know what was inside?

SIERRA Eeeeuw, what?

RACHEL This isn't true. There aren't cannibals in *Africa*. Cannibals are somewhere else, an island, I think.

PERSEPHONE No way. Africa.

RACHEL My dad *said*.

PERSEPHONE Africa.

RACHEL *No!*

SIERRA Mama, where are cannibals? Are they on an island?

MAX Are they *here*?

JANE I don't—

PERSEPHONE Whatever! Don't you want to hear the rest of the story?

SIERRA Yes!

MAX *No!*

RACHEL It's not *true* . . .

PERSEPHONE So she took off her hat and opened up her present. And it was fingers! And ears!

(MAX *slams his hands over his ears.*)

MAX Scary!

SIERRA Eeeeeeuww!!!

RACHEL Stupid . . .

PERSEPHONE And eyeballs! And little toenails! And *that's* what she found! They liked her so much they gave her all of their favorite things! It was really a nice present, if you think about it.

(*Pause.*)

JANE And then what? What did she do with all the fingers and ears and eyeballs? Did she keep them? Did she send them back? Did she eat them? Did she dip them in Lucite as a memory of her big adventure?

PERSEPHONE . . . I don't know. That's the end of the story. I don't know what she did.

JANE Oh. Well. Here we are. (*She stops the car at the school.*) Everybody out.

Little Airplanes of the Heart

2000

>STEVE FEFFER

ORIGINAL PRODUCTION

DIRECTOR Eliza Beckwith

SET DESIGNER Warren Karp

COSTUME DESIGNER Amela Baksic

SOUND Beatrice Terry

PROPS Cynthia Franks

PRODUCTION STAGE MANAGER John Thornberry

The cast was as follows:

UNCLE JOHN William Wise

SAM A. J. Shively

JILLY Shayna Levine

LORRAINE Elaine Bromka

CHERYL Ann Talman

FARMER JOHN/PRINCIPAL BECKER/THE RABBI Peter Lewis

CHARACTERS

UNCLE JOHN mid-fifties

SAM John's nephew, age twelve

JILLY John's daughter, around the same age as Sam

LORRAINE Sam's mother

CHERYL John's wife

FARMER JOHN/PRINCIPAL BECKER/THE RABBI one male actor

PLACE

Cape Cod, Massachusetts, and from Cape Cod en route to Montana

TIME

The present

> "The little airplanes of the heart
> with their brave little propellers
> What can they do
> against the winds of darkness
> even as butterflies are beaten back
> by hurricanes
> yet do not die."
>
> —LAWRENCE FERLINGHETTI

Lights up on SAM's *house and* UNCLE JOHN's *homemade plane.* UNCLE JOHN *is a significantly overweight man in his mid-fifties squeezed into both seats of an ultra-light, single-propeller plane. The plane is suspended from*

above the stage over the rest of the action. It remains there for the duration
of the play. The plane has been painted bright yellow and says CHERYL *in*
small letters on the side. UNCLE JOHN *wears a scarf, a headset, and a*
leather jacket. Sounds of the plane in flight are heard. Sounds of the wind.
UNCLE JOHN's *scarf is blowing out behind him as he "maneuvers" the plane.*

Lights up on SAM. *He stands below* UNCLE JOHN's *plane. He holds a*
small yellow toy plane. He addresses the audience.

SAM My Uncle John built an ultra-light airplane. He built it in
the basement of our house on Cape Cod, and he flew it all the
way to a dairy farm in Grassy Butte, North Dakota.
Unfortunately he was trying to fly to an airport in Sydney,
Montana, which was seventy miles farther. It was my Uncle
John's dream to build a plane and fly it to Montana. *(He looks up
at* UNCLE JOHN.*)* Why Montana, Uncle John?

UNCLE JOHN *(Over the wind and the plane engine)* Because it's so
magnificent.

SAM But it's 1998. There are roads that go there. Or big jets.

UNCLE JOHN I know, but it's not the same. Montana is "big sky"
country, and it's from outta the big sky that I wanna approach
it.

SAM *(To the audience)* Uncle John built his plane in our basement
because he lived in a ranch house. He thought that building the
plane was something that he and his brother, my father, could
do. My father never got interested, and subsequently he died of
a heart attack two years before Uncle John attempted his
Montana flight. Everyone in the family thought that it was
Uncle John who would die first, on account of his weight, but it
didn't work out that way. Uncle John had to have the wall of
our basement removed so he could get his plane out. My mother
once said, "They need to remove the wall to get John out."

UNCLE JOHN *(Over the wind and plane noise)* I thought the plane was something your father and I would futz around with—may he rest in peace. But damn if that plane and that state didn't start to get under my skin. Big-sky country from outta the big sky. I worked on it a little each day, and before I knew it, the plane was finished.

SAM Other people in the family thought that Uncle John was crazy, but I could spend hours helping him.

(JILLY enters. She wears a plaid skirt and a green blouse that look like a school uniform.)

JILLY My father's crazy, you know?

SAM No, he's not.

JILLY Are you going to stay down here all night and watch him?

SAM I help him.

JILLY No, you don't. You just sit there and watch him. I think maybe *you're* crazy.

SAM I'm interested.

JILLY If you're interested in what a crazy person does, then you must be crazy.

SAM Uncle John is going to take me with him to Montana because I'm so helpful.

JILLY Where you gonna fit?

SAM Uncle John is a genius. He'll find a way.

JILLY You'd go up in that thing? Now I know you're crazy.

SAM You won't think we're so crazy when Uncle John and I get to Montana.

JILLY I'm bored. Come upstairs with me.

SAM No thanks.

JILLY My mother and Auntie Lorraine said that you're supposed to play with me.

SAM Can't. Gotta help Uncle John.

JILLY I'll lift up my skirt and show you my underpants if you'll come upstairs and play with me.

SAM Uncle's John putting on a wing. We got them delivered yesterday in a huge box that took two big men to carry.

JILLY You really are crazy. (*She lifts up her plaid skirt and shows* SAM *her underpants.*) I see London and I see France. Crazy Cousin Sam can see my underpants.

(JILLY *stands with her skirt up for a beat.* SAM *looks at her, confused.*)

UNCLE JOHN (*Over the wind and airplane noise*) The first wings that I put on had to be sent back. They weren't big enough on account of all the weight I added to the plane. And, of course, all the weight I had put on. (*He chuckles.*) But these new wings should do it.

(JILLY *puts her skirt down.*)

JILLY (*To* UNCLE JOHN) Why can't you play golf like other daddies?

(JILLY *exits. The lights change.*)

SAM My mother used to tell me that I needed a hobby like my Uncle John's.

(LORRAINE *enters.*)

LORRAINE Having too much time on one's hands is a dangerous thing

SAM But since Uncle John's flight, she doesn't say that anymore.

LORRAINE There are all sorts of other hobbies for a boy your age. Baseball-card collecting. Stamp collecting. Butterfly collecting.

SAM I wanna build a plane in our basement and fly it over the farm in North Dakota where Uncle John went down.

LORRAINE I never wanna hear you say another word about planes or basements or Montana.

SAM North Dakota.

LORRAINE Whatever. It's sick! Do you wanna leave your family like your Uncle John did?

SAM He didn't leave.

LORRAINE Then what happened to him?

SAM He had an accident.

LORRAINE He senselessly wasted his life and left your cousin Jilly without a daddy and your Auntie Cheryl without a husband. He even left you without an Uncle John, didn't he?

SAM He's still my Uncle John.

LORRAINE In spirit, of course, he'll always be your uncle. But wouldn't it have been nice if he could be here now? Don't you wish he hadn't built that plane and attempted that crazy flight to North Dakota?

SAM Montana.

LORRAINE Whatever. I bet your Uncle John wishes he could be here with you.

SAM I bet he wished he had made it to Montana.

LORRAINE The point is: Unlike your father, your Uncle John never learned to be a realist. A 295-pound man should have better sense than to squeeze into an ultra-light plane and fly it to Montana when he has a beautiful wife and child. When you have a wife and child of your own, you'll understand this.

SAM If having a wife and child means not flying to North Dakota to see where Uncle John went down, then I'm never gonna have 'em.

LORRAINE That's what you say now. But when you're a big boy you'll meet someone who'll make you feel differently.

SAM Never. *(He pretends to fly his plane.)* Next stop Grassy Butte, North Dakota.

LORRAINE I told you, Sam: no planes, no basements, and no North Dakota! If you don't stop it, I will take that away from you.

*(*LORRAINE *exits. The lights change. During the motion of landing his toy*

plane, SAM *takes out a pen and begins to write a letter. As* SAM *speaks,* FARMER JOHN *enters.)*

SAM Dear Mr. Farmer John: Hello to you. My name is Sam. I am twelve years old. My Uncle John crashed the plane that he built in my basement into your dairy farm in Grassy Butte, North Dakota. I'm writing to ask you the following questions in regards to my Uncle John. (1) How did you feel when you heard that the man whose plane dropped onto your farm had the same name as you? (2) Were any animals hurt in the crash?. . .

FARMER JOHN *(Continuing* SAM*'s letter)* (3) Do you have a son, and if so, how old is he? (4) Could I come and visit you this summer? (5) Did you happen to find a good-luck card that I made for my Uncle John and that I gave to him before his flight? I would like it for my Uncle John scrapbook. I look forward to your answers. Please say hello to Mrs. Farmer John and any Farmer John children you might have—see question 3 . . .

SAM Sincerely, Sam, Uncle John's nephew and honorary co-pilot.

FARMER JOHN Dear Sam: It was very nice to hear from you. My family and I are so sorry about the tragic loss of your Uncle John. From all we've heard he was a remarkable man and a great, brave adventurer. Though we didn't know him, we think of him often, particularly during planting and harvest time, when we're out in that corner of the field. Now called Uncle John's Field in your Uncle John's honor. In answer to your questions: (1) I hadn't really thought about it too much that his name's John and my name's John. But now that you mention it, it does make me feel like I know him a little better. (2) No, none of our animals were hurt in the crash. Even with the tremendous explosion, it was still quite far away from our farm buildings. I suppose a wild animal like a field mouse or rabbit might've been hurt, but I'm guessing that's not what you mean.

SAM *(Continuing* FARMER JOHN's *letter)* (3) Yes, I do have a son. He's twelve years old. I also have a daughter, age fifteen. (4) If it's okay with your mother and father, of course you can come out and visit. Just let us know. (5) No, no good-luck card was recovered. As you may have heard, there was a great deal of fire and it is highly unlikely that any paper would've survived such an inferno . . .

FARMER JOHN *(Continuing the letter)* However, one never knows, and we'll keep looking. Again, let me say how sorry my whole family is about your loss. We pray that God delivers peace to him and all of you. Sincerely yours, Farmer John.

(The lights change. SAM *flies the toy yellow plane across the stage. It lands on a table that is made up for Thanksgiving.* SAM *parks the toy plane next to a large turkey sitting uncarved on the table.* LORRAINE, JILLY, *and* CHERYL *are seated around the table.)*

LORRAINE Get that off the table, Sam.

SAM It's a decoration.

LORRAINE I said, get it off.

CHERYL That's all right, Lor. I know Sam is just showing his love for his Uncle John.

LORRAINE He shouldn't have toys on the table.

SAM It's not a toy. It's a model.

LORRAINE Whatever it is, get it off.

*(*SAM *pretends that the plane takes off from the table, and he lands it under the chair that he sits on.)*

JILLY Why aren't Sam and I sitting at the kids' table?

CHERYL Because there's no kids' table this year.

JILLY Why not?

CHERYL Thanksgiving's just a little gathering this year. And besides, you always complain when you have to sit at the kids' table.

JILLY I know, but this is lame; it's just like a regular dinner.

LORRAINE It's not a regular dinner; it's special 'cause we're all together.

SAM Not Uncle John.

CHERYL In spirit, your Uncle John is with us. Just like in spirit your father is with us . . .

SAM I got a letter yesterday from Farmer John and he said I could come visit this summer.

CHERYL Who?

LORRAINE Sam . . .

SAM The dairy farmer in North Dakota.

LORRAINE I forgot that his name was John.

SAM They had the same name.

JILLY So do a lot of people . . .

SAM He said that I can come and visit him in North Dakota. He has a boy my age and also a daughter.

JILLY Can I go?

SAM No.

JILLY Why not?

SAM 'Cause I'm gonna build a plane and fly there, and you called that crazy . . .

JILLY My mom can drive me there . . .

LORRAINE Sam, Jilly, please. First of all, Sam is not going to North Dakota.

JILLY See . . . Crazy, woo-woo . . . Just like my daddy . . .

CHERYL Jilly . . .

SAM I'm going . . .

LORRAINE Sam, what did I tell you about that?

CHERYL No, no, Lor, it's okay . . . I understand Sam's curiosity. The truth is, Sam, there's not much to see. It's just a cornfield. And all this corn is so tall that I couldn't even see what little was left of the plane. Not that I wanted to.

LORRAINE Why are we talking about this?

CHERYL Really, it's okay. I can save Sam a trip. The funny thing is, there's not much difference between Sydney, Montana, and Grassy Butte, North Dakota. John might just as well have tried to land in North Dakota instead of seventy miles farther in Montana.

SAM He didn't dream of North Dakota. He dreamed of Montana.

CHERYL Well, he might as well have dreamed of North Dakota, because it was the same goddamn dream. The same goddamn cornfields. The same goddamn road. The same goddamn farm-houses. I know, because I drove from Montana to North Dakota with his dental records to identify what was left of his goddamn body.

JILLY Mommy swore . . .

LORRAINE Enough! I don't wanna hear any more about it! We're gonna carve the turkey and we're gonna talk about all the things we have to be thankful for. *(There's quiet for a moment.)* Now, who's gonna carve?

SAM *(Quietly)* I know they're not the same. Sydney and Grassy Butte. Montana and North Dakota. I know it. 'Cause I have the same dream. Uncle John's dream.

(The lights change.)

UNCLE JOHN *(Over the wind and plane noise)* I'm not sure you can understand this, Sam, and I'm almost embarrassed to say it, but when I'm in this plane, the feeling is very sexual. There's not much room between me and the engine, and it gives off the most remarkable vibrations. I once actually had a . . . a . . . very special feeling during the flight. The kind of feeling that I hope your father explained to you while he was alive, and if not, that you'll find out about sooner or later in the schoolyard. It was right after takeoff. I don't think I was much out of

Massachusetts. It didn't even have to do with sex. I felt so full of joy that I was flying toward my dream that it just took me by surprise. However, let me add that in no way did this contribute to the crash. I was not having . . . such a feeling at the time the old Volkswagen engine began to make the first sounds of trouble. *(Lights change.* SAM *is sitting on one of those children's rides of various shapes {usually horses or cars} that are frequently outside convenience stores and five-and-dimes {in New York, anyway} and that, after a quarter is put in, play music and move up and down in a rocking motion.* SAM *is on one shaped like an airplane. A red sign behind him says* WOOLWORTH *and there are various signs announcing sale items. The ride ends.* SAM *puts another quarter in. The lights change. In the middle of the ride,* LORRAINE *enters with* PRINCIPAL BECKER.*)*

LORRAINE I know you don't want to tell me where you were, but why not tell Principal Becker?

PRINCIPAL BECKER We're concerned, Sam, not only because you've been missing school, but because you won't tell us where you've been. Now, you know it's not safe to be wandering around by yourself.

SAM It seems safe.

PRINCIPAL BECKER It may seem safe, and certainly the Cape is, for the most part, a nice safe place to grow up in. But it's not safe by yourself, and not when we don't know where you are.

SAM Is it safer than flying to Montana in a plane you built by yourself?

PRINCIPAL BECKER Well, now that depends on where you were wandering . . .

LORRAINE However, I think Principal Becker would agree that each is stupid in its own way. It is stupid for a 295-pound man to fly an ultra-light plane to North Dakota . . .

SAM Montana . . .

LORRAINE Whatever. And it's stupid for a little boy to be out wandering in West Yarmouth when he's supposed to be in school.

PRINCIPAL BECKER We don't like to say *stupid* . . .

LORRAINE What do you like to say?

PRINCIPAL BECKER Not smart.

LORRAINE A 295-pound man flying in an ultra-light plane to Montana is *stupid*.

PRINCIPAL BECKER But what Sam did is *not smart*.

LORRAINE We don't know that because we don't know where he was.

PRINCIPAL BECKER Now, Sam, why would a boy who gets high marks in school such as yourself be out wandering around away from the classroom?

SAM I wasn't wandering.

PRINCIPAL BECKER Then what were you doing?

SAM I was practicing.

PRINCIPAL BECKER Practicing what?

SAM For my trip to North Dakota.

LORRAINE You're not going to North Dakota.

SAM I took her for some spins around the Cape to see how she feels.

UNCLE JOHN (*Above the wind and the airplane noise*) And damn if she isn't soft, Sammy-boy.

SAM Like a cloud with wings.

UNCLE JOHN You'd think she was one of those big birds.

SAM The new wings make all the difference.

UNCLE JOHN And having all this weight is gonna be a blessing in disguise. I'm like a built-in stabilizer.

SAM I thought I'd have to stop maybe four or five times a day 'cause of the rough flyin', but now . . .

UNCLE JOHN AND SAM I think I'll be able to make it to Montana in two or three days.

(*As* SAM *and* UNCLE JOHN *complete the following,* SAM's *ride is coming to an end. The music and plane slow down.*)

PRINCIPAL BECKER Now, Sam, everyone knows that an imagination is a good thing. Lord knows that we encourage it here at Kennedy School. But there is worktime and playtime. Now, you must learn to be realistic and separate the two.

(*The lights change.*)

UNCLE JOHN (*Over the wind and plane sounds*) I thought about your old man a lot during my flight. Boy, did I love him, Sam. I wish he would've taken more of an interest in the plane, but, you know, that's not like him. Owning your own drugstore like that is a lot of work and he didn't have time to futz around with me. I'll tell you what, though: I bet I would've gotten him up here. Oh yes. I can picture it. You know what he once said to me, Sam? It was one of the few times I could get him down in the basement to work on the plane. He was having a great time, and he said that he would've liked to spend more time with us. He really did. And then he said, "I hope my son doesn't go into retail. I know a lot of fathers want their sons to follow in their footsteps, but I think Sam would be better off doing something else." That's not an easy thing for a father to say. But he always wanted what was best for you. Sometimes during my journey I imagined that your dad was flying with me. I'd point out to him all the incredible things that I was experiencing, and it made the experience more vivid for me. Your dad was one of us, Sam, even though he didn't always show it. He had his head in the clouds, and don't let your mother tell you otherwise.

(*The lights change.* SAM *flies his toy yellow plane across the stage. He lands it in front of the newly replaced wall of his basement.* SAM *begins to feel the wall with his hands. Behind him is a bumper pool table that he doesn't acknowledge.* LORRAINE *enters. She watches him for a few beats.* SAM *sits in front of the wall.*)

LORRAINE The builder said that we would save an extra fifty dollars a month in heating costs now that our basement has four walls again.

SAM How am I going to get my plane out?

LORRAINE This isn't an airplane hangar; it's a basement.

SAM It makes the basement look funny.

LORRAINE No, it makes the basement look normal. When your Uncle John turned it into an airport, then it looked funny. (SAM *continues to study the wall, as* LORRAINE *crosses to the bumper pool table.*) Hey, did you see what I got you?

SAM No.

LORRAINE It's a bumper pool table.

(SAM *turns around.*)

SAM A what?

LORRAINE (*As she takes a shot*) A bumper pool table.

SAM Where am I going to put the wing assembly?

LORRAINE I thought maybe you'd want to play with it until you got started on your plane. You know, you're becoming a big boy. Soon you'll be having your bar mitzvah. You're gonna want a place where you can play with your friends.

SAM Bumper pool?

LORRAINE Before he died, your dad dreamed of turning this basement into a rec room. He thought it'd be fun for you as you got older. He wanted to put in video games and a TV and a pool table. Things like that. Perhaps a place for both of you. But you know your father. He had a big heart. He couldn't say no to anyone. John wanted to move his plane in, and of course your father said yes.

SAM His big heart just stopped.

LORRAINE Yes, it did.

SAM Like the Volkswagen engine.

LORRAINE What?

SAM That Uncle John had in the *Cheryl*. Sometimes it'd just stop.

LORRAINE C'mon, try it. (*She takes another shot.*) It's fun.

(SAM *crosses over with the plane. He tries to land it on the felt. The plane hits one of the bumpers and flips over. The lights change.*)

UNCLE JOHN (*Over the wind and the plane noises*) When I got to North Dakota, I really thought I was going to make it. I was actually comfortable for the first time during the journey. I was imagining what I would say to Cheryl when I saw her at the Sydney, Montana, airport. You know, all sorts of funny comments. I had finally decided on one about no longer paying the premiums on that special life insurance she made me take out.

(*The lights change.* SAM *lands his plane at the feet of* JILLY, CHERYL, *and* LORRAINE, *who are all wearing black. It is* UNCLE JOHN's *funeral. A* RABBI *is speaking.*)

RABBI We may not know where he is, but like Jonah in the belly of the whale, he will not escape the sight of God. He was not Ulysses or Jason of Argonaut fame. He was a Jew. A man not destined for heroic and great adventures or wanderings. A good man. A *mensch*. A simple *mensch* on this earth who brought laughter to those who knew him, a quality product to those who bought his linoleum tiles, and love to his family and friends. Uncle John, though your body is lost, you are not lost in the sight of your God. As you are not lost in the eyes of your friends and family on this earth. Please recite with me.

RABBI AND MOURNERS *Yit-ga-dol vi'yit-ka-dash sh'may ra-bo, B'ol-mo dee-v'ro chir-u-tay, v'yam-leech mal-chu-tay . . .*

(*The lights change.*)

SAM Everyone was so proud of Jilly because she didn't cry at the funeral. My mother said she was a strong little girl. I cried like a little baby. Be strong, my mother said. Your cousin Jilly is going to need you.

(Lights up on JILLY. *She is wearing her black dress.)*

JILLY Watcha doin' in the basement?

SAM I'm thinkin'.

JILLY What about?

SAM It looks funny without Uncle John's plane.

JILLY I told you he was crazy.

SAM It's not nice to say that about him after he's dead.

JILLY He's my dad. Dead or not, I can say anything I want about him, and I say he was crazy.

SAM Shhh. My mother says he can hear us.

JILLY So. He knows he's crazy. Look what happened to him. I bet all the way down he thought to himself, I'm crazy. I'm crazy. I'm a crazy dad!

(Lights up on UNCLE JOHN.*)*

UNCLE JOHN *(Over the wind and the airplane noises)* I never felt so alive. Even after the old Volkswagen engine sputtered out completely, I didn't think, Oh, this was a mistake, John. You shouldn't have done this. I thought, Wow, I just really lived. I would like to live more like this. Unfortunately, I probably won't have the chance now. And then, of course, I thought, Damn, I wish I had lost that twenty pounds so I had room for a parachute.

JILLY *(Yelling at the plane above the stage)* Crazy, crazy, crazy dad!

SAM You're crazy for yelling at a dead person.

JILLY Your mother said that you have to be nice to me on account of my dad dying.

SAM I'm trying.

JILLY You want me to lift up my funeral dress and show you my underpants?

(SAM *looks at* JILLY *and then in the direction of where* UNCLE JOHN *was building the plane in the now empty basement. He then looks back at* JILLY.)

SAM I guess so.

(JILLY *pulls up her funeral dress. The lights go out on* JILLY.)

SAM When I'm old enough to go to Grassy Butte, North Dakota, by myself, I will. I'll fly there in a plane that I made in this very basement. I'll find Farmer John's field, and when I fly over it, white plumes of smoke will shoot out the back of my plane and form the words "Uncle John Was Here" exclamation point. And after a low pass over the field where I will tip my wings to Farmer John and his family, I will make it that final seventy miles to Montana. I will make it for my Uncle John. Outta the big sky into big-sky country.

UNCLE JOHN (*Over the wind and the sounds of his engine sputtering, as he struggles to control his plane*) Why Montana, Sam?

SAM Because it's so magnificent.

UNCLE JOHN (*Over the sounds of his engine sputtering even worse and the plane taking more effort to control*) You know, it's 1998; they have roads that go to Montana. Or big jets.

SAM I know, but it's not the same.

(UNCLE JOHN *continues to try to control the plane and its sputtering engine, before it stops completely. The sound of the wind rises, as the lights slowly fade on* UNCLE JOHN. *There remains a soft spotlight on* UNCLE JOHN'*s peaceful face and a light on* SAM, *who is bringing his toy plane down for a safe landing. The sound of a crash is* not *heard. The lights fade.*)

Lives of the Saints

2000

> DAVID IVES

ORIGINAL EST PRODUCTION

DIRECTOR John Rando
SET DESIGNER Chris Jones
COSTUME DESIGNER Julie Doyle
SOUND Robert Gould
PROPS Laura Raynor
PRODUCTION STAGE MANAGER Jim Ring
STAGE MANAGER James Carringer
ART DIRECTION Sara Garonzik

The cast was as follows:
EDNA Nancy Opel
FLO Anne O'Sullivan
STAGEHAND Sean Sutherland
STAGEHAND Chris Wight

This play was originally produced by the Philadelphia Theatre
Company in 1998.

CHARACTERS

EDNA
FLO
STAGEHAND
STAGEHAND

PLACE

A kitchen in a church basement

TIME

The present

> *This play is dedicated to my mother, Regina Roszkowski. Vivat!*
> *Vivat Regina!*

Totally bare stage—which will remain totally bare and totally propless and furnitureless until noted. EDNA *enters up right and* FLO *enters up left, as if through swinging doors we do not see. There is a momentary burst of distant church music as they enter, as if we are overhearing music from where they came from.* EDNA *and* FLO *wear ancient flowered housedresses, spotless aprons, and loudly flapping, flattened slippers. Each carries something in her arms which we do not see. They cross, passing each other.*

EDNA You got da candle'ss, Flo?
FLO I got da candle'ss. You got da doilese?
EDNA I got da St. Stanislas Kostka doilese.
FLO Oll do da utensil'ss.
EDNA Oll do da plate'ss.

(They exit, EDNA up left, FLO up right, again to that momentary burst of distant church music. They re-enter immediately and cross back.)

EDNA Opp, dat's da wrong side.

FLO Opp, dat's da wrong side.

EDNA What'm I tinkin . . .

FLO What'm I tinkin . . .

(They exit, EDNA up left, FLO up right. Offstage we hear the noise of a hundred rattled utensils and a hundred clattering plates. EDNA and FLO re-enter—again we hear that momentary burst of church music—wiping their hands on their aprons, their slippers flapping loudly.)

EDNA Okay, so we put out utensil'ss . . .

FLO An we put out da plate'ss . . .

EDNA Da candle'ss have ta be lit.

FLO An we got da St. Stanislas Kostka doilese.

(EDNA heads counterclockwise, FLO clockwise, as if around a table at center we do not see. EDNA goes to a "stove" at left, which we do not see, and stirs a "pot," while FLO goes to a "sideboard" at right and turns on an electric "handmixer." We hear its motor go VRRRR. She stops the "mixer" and the VRRRR stops. EDNA taps a "wooden spoon" on the side of a "pot" three times, and we hear the TAP, TAP, TAP. Then she "stirs" again as FLO runs the "handmixer" and we hear the VRRRR. FLO stops the invisible mixer— the VRRRR stops—and EDNA bangs the "wooden spoon" three times as we hear the TAP, TAP, TAP.

The two women move down center, where side by side each woman turns a squeaking "tap" and we hear the squeak of the tap and the water running as they "wash their hands" under a stream of "water" not apparent to us.)

EDNA Now dat was a very nice funeral.

FLO Wasn't dat a beautyful funeral.

EDNA I wouldn't mind having dat.

FLO I wouldn't mind having dat for my funeral.

EDNA But I will tell you a song I do not want sung at *my* funeral.
Da teme from *Da Phantom of da Opera* is not appropriate.

FLO An not "Is That All There Is" needer.

EDNA Omm traditional, Flo.

FLO Edna, Omm traditional, too.

(We hear the DING! *of a kitchen timer.)*

EDNA Opp, dere's da cake.

(They each turn a squeaking "tap" and the water sound stops.)

FLO Oll check da Jell-O mold'ss.

EDNA Oll check da cake.

*(*EDNA *circles toward left,* FLO *toward right, their slippers flapping loudly as they wipe their hands on their aprons.)*

FLO Ha we doin' fer time?

EDNA We got until da cemetery an back.

FLO Plenny a time.

EDNA Plenny a time. *(At left* EDNA *opens an "oven door," which we do not see. We hear its metallic groan and she bends to look in.* FLO *at right opens a "refrigerator door" we do not see, and a "refrigerator" light shines on her as she looks in.)* Fi'e more minutes.

FLO Fi'e more minutes.

*(*EDNA *closes the "oven door" and we hear its metallic creak and bang, while* FLO *closes the "refrigerator" and the "refrigerator" light goes out.)*

EDNA *(Pointing to a "dish" on a "sideboard" we don't see)* Okay, sa we did da patayta salad . . .

FLO *(Pointing to another "dish" on a "sideboard")* Da green salad . . .

EDNA *(Pointing elsewhere)* Fruit salad.

FLO *(Pointing elsewhere)* Coleslaw.

EDNA *(Pointing to a "table" at center we do not see)* Der's da apple slices.

FLO *(Pointing to "table")* Nut clusters.

EDNA *(Pointing to "table")* Cheesecake.

FLO (*Pointing to "oven"*) Pond cake, crumb cake, angel food.

EDNA (*Pointing to "sideboard"*) Krooshcheeki.

FLO (*Pointing elsewhere*) Kolachki.

EDNA (*Pointing to "table"*) Krooler'ss.

FLO (*Pointing to "refrigerator"*) Jell-O.

EDNA (*Pointing to "stove"*) An prune'ss.

FLO For twelve people?

EDNA I tink it's enough.

FLO (*Heading for "sideboard" at right*) Der used to be pot holders down here with St. Damien an da lepers.

EDNA (*Heading for "stove" at left*) Odda know what happened to dose lepers. (*She stirs a "pot" on the "stove" we do not see at left, while shaking in "salt." We hear the sprinkling of the salt. She stops.* FLO *at a "counter" at right turns on the "handmixer."* VRRRR. *She stops the "mixer" and* EDNA *beats a "wooden spoon" three times on the edge of a "pot."* TAP, TAP, TAP.) Plus we got da sossitch.

FLO Der's da sossitch.

(EDNA *sprinkles another "pot."* SPRINKLE—*stop.* VRRRR—*stop.* TAP, TAP, TAP.)

EDNA Der's da chicken wit Campbell's mushroom scup.

FLO Der's da perogi.

EDNA Da perogi, da gawoomki.

(*SPRINKLE—stop.* VRRRR—*stop.* TAP, TAP, TAP.)

FLO Der's kapoosta.

EDNA Da roll'ss, da bun'ss, an da bread.

FLO An da Polish glazed ham.

(*SPRINKLE—stop.* VRRRR—*stop.* TAP, TAP, TAP.)

EDNA For twelve people . . . ?

FLO I tink it's enough. (*She carries the "bowl" she was just mixing to the "table" at center.*)

EDNA Don't put dat der, Flo, it's dirty.

FLO Is it dirty?

EDNA Yeah, it's dirty. *(She sweeps "crumbs" from the "table" into her hand and we hear the brushing sound, then* FLO *sets down the "bowl."* EDNA *throws the "crumbs" into the "sink" down center.)*

EDNA Oll do da poddered sugar.

FLO Oll do da nuts.

(Wiping their hands on their aprons, their slippers flapping loudly, EDNA *goes to high "cabinets" at left,* FLO *to a bank of "drawers" at left.)*

EDNA Okay, wurr's da poddered sugar . . .

FLO Okay, wurr's da nuts . . .

EDNA Poddered sugar . . . *(She opens a "cabinet." We hear it SQUEAK. She looks in.)*

FLO Nuts . . .

*(*FLO *opens a "drawer" and we hear its wooden CREAK.* EDNA *closes cabinet: SQUEAK and BANG.)*

EDNA Poddered sugar . . .

*(*EDNA *opens another "cabinet": SQUEAK.* FLO *closes "drawer": RATTLE and BANG.)*

FLO Nuts . . .

*(*EDNA *closes "cabinet": SQUEAK and BANG.* FLO *opens "drawer": WOODEN CREAK.)*

EDNA Fodder Tom says to me, Edna, wouldja do a funeral breakfast fer Mary, I couldn't find nobody.

FLO I say to um, Fodder, I cooked so many meals in dis church bazement . . .

EDNA I'm *happy* to.

*(*EDNA *opens "cabinet": SQUEAK.* FLO *closes "drawer": RATTLE and BANG.)*

FLO I might's well *live* in dis church bazement.

EDNA I says, Mary'll need some substenance.

FLO *(Opens "drawer": CREAK.)* Edna and me'll throw somethin together.

EDNA *(Finding it.)* Opp! Da poddered sugar. *(She closes "cabinet":* SQUEAK *and* BANG.*)*

FLO Opp! Da nuts.

*(*FLO *closes "drawer":* RATTLE *and* BANG. *The two women go to the "table" at center.)*

EDNA Oh, da tings dat Mary has been t'rough.

FLO Oh, da tragedy innat family.

EDNA Just terrible. *(She sprinkles "powdered sugar" from a "can" onto a "dessert." We hear* SPRINKLE, SPRINKLE, SPRINKLE.*)*

FLO Just terrible. *(She turns the "crank" of a "nut grinder" over another "dessert." We hear the grinding.)* An you know Barney didn't leave her nuttin.

EDNA I always tought Barney was gonna come to a bad end wid alla dat drinkin. *(She sprinkles "powdered sugar" onto another "dessert."* SPRINKLE, SPRINKLE, SPRINKLE.*)*

FLO Run over by his own lawn mower.

EDNA Just terrible.

FLO Just terrible.

(Simultaneously, EDNA *sprinkles "powdered sugar" while* FLO *turns the "crank" of the "grinder."* SPRINKLE, SPRINKLE, SPRINKLE. GRIND, GRIND, GRIND. *They stop simultaneously. During this, the back wall opens up and we see two* STAGEHANDS *who are at a table doing all the sound effects.* EDNA *and* FLO *do not acknowledge them.)*

EDNA I'm prayin to St. Jude fer Mary.

FLO Patron saint a lost causes.

EDNA Jude'll bring her somethin.

FLO You remember what St. Jude did fer me when I had piles.

EDNA He brought you dat special ointment.

FLO A miracle.

*(*SPRINKLE, SPRINKLE, SPRINKLE. GRIND, GRIND, GRIND. *They stop simultaneously, then* EDNA *heads left and* FLO *heads right.)*

EDNA Ya know, when Joe died, Mary made me sixteen ponds a perogi. *(She opens a "cabinet"—SQUEAK—and puts away the "powdered-sugar can.")*

FLO When Stosh died, Mary gay'me a twenty-two-pond turkey. *(She opens a "drawer"—WOODEN CREAK—and puts away the "nut grinder.")*

EDNA So der's justice in da world.

FLO So der's some justice.

(Simultaneously EDNA closes the "cabinet" and FLO closes the "drawer"—SQUEAK, BANG, BANG.)

EDNA *(Heading down center)* Too bad we couldn't go ta da cemetery.

FLO *(Heading down center)* For Mary's sake.

(As before, side by side each woman turns a squeaky "tap" and we hear the water running as they "wash their hands" under a stream of "water" not apparent to us.)

EDNA St. Casimir's my favorite cemetery, too.

FLO Just beautyful.

EDNA Da way dey take care a da grave'ss der.

FLO Da grave'ss are always like noo.

EDNA An da bat'rooms.

FLO Spotless.

EDNA I just pre-ordered my casket from dat place in Blue Island.

FLO I got my casket. Didja get da blue coffin wit satin?

EDNA I got da pink wit chiffon.

FLO Just beautyful.

EDNA Just beautyful.

(Each turns a "tap" and the water sound stops.)

FLO I bought some patayta chips.

EDNA I bought some taco chips.

(Wiping their hands on their aprons, they move to "paper bags" on the floor and we hear the CRINKLE of cellophane bags as they go through them.)

FLO Patayta chips . . .

EDNA Taco chips . . .

FLO Patayta chips . . .

EDNA Taco chips . . .

(They stop. CRINKLE stops, too.)

FLO Ya tink chips are appropriate fer a funeral breakfast?

EDNA Maybe not for breakfast.

FLO Not for breakfast.

(DING! of a kitchen timer.)

EDNA AND FLO Opp!

FLO Ya wanna check da Jell-O?

EDNA Ya wanna check da cake?

(Slippers flapping loudly, wiping their hands on their aprons, FLO moves left, and EDNA moves right.)

FLO I was gonna make duck-blood soup wit raisins and dumplings. But you know da problem wit makin duck-blood soup no more.

EDNA You can't find no duck blood.

FLO Der's no duck blood.

(FLO opens the "oven door"—METALLIC CREAK—as EDNA opens the "refrigerator door"—the "refrigerator" light goes on. They look in.)

EDNA My ma use ta kill da ducks herself in da garotch.

FLO You know it's not da killin.

EDNA It's when dey urinate all over you.

FLO Just terrible.

EDNA Just terrible.

FLO Cake's done.

EDNA Jell-O's done.

(FLO closes the "oven door"—METALLIC CREAK and BANG—as EDNA closes the "refrigerator door"—"refrigerator" light goes out.)

FLO It's da same ting wit makin pickled pigs' feet.

EDNA Der's no feet. (FLO *"sprinkles salt" into a pot. SPRINKLE,*
SPRINKLE, SPRINKLE. EDNA shakes a "can of whipped cream" and we
hear the shaking can. She stops, and FLO bangs a "wooden spoon" three
times on the edge of a "pot": BANG, BANG, BANG.) I toldja I lost doze
feet I bought in Blue Island.

FLO Did you pray to St. Ant'ny?

EDNA I prayed to St. Ant'ny. Two days later I found um.

FLO Were da feet in de izebox?

EDNA Da feet were in de izebox alla time.

(FLO sighs. EDNA sighs. FLO "sprinkles salt" into a "pot": SPRINKLE,
SPRINKLE, SPRINKLE. She stops and EDNA shakes the "whipped cream can":
SHAKE, SHAKE, SHAKE.)

EDNA Wit da whip' cream, should I do da rosettes or da
squiggle'ss?

FLO I tink rosettes.

EDNA Rosettes . . . ? Fine.

(Simultaneously, FLO SPRINKLES and EDNA SHAKES. They stop
simultaneously.)

FLO Or maybe rosettes in da middle . . .

EDNA . . . squiggle'ss on da side.

FLO Squiggle'ss on da side.

(FLO SPRINKLES, then stops. EDNA sprays some "whipped cream" onto a
"dessert" on the "table" center and we hear the PFFFLLL of the nozzle. She
stops. FLO bangs a "wooden spoon" on the edge of a "pot." BANG, BANG,
BANG. They repeat that once, then FLO starts humming a tune, using the
"whipped cream" spurts to mark the rhythm. EDNA joins in, humming,
using the SPRINKLES of "salt" and the "wooden spoon's" BANGS. Pretty soon
this has developed into the "Beer Barrel Polka" and they're really going at
it, banging on the "table" we don't see, tapping on the side of the "stove"
that isn't apparent to us. When they stop, EDNA sighs. FLO sighs.)

EDNA Ya know Fodder Tom tol me a joke today.

FLO Oh yeah?

(PFFFLLL.)

EDNA What's it say onna bottom a Polish Coca-Cola bottles?

FLO What's it say onna bottom a Polish Coca-Cola bottles . . .

EDNA Onna bottom a Polish Coca-Cola bottles.

FLO I give up.

EDNA "Open Udder End."

(They laugh. SPRINKLE, SPRINKLE, SPRINKLE. PFFFLLL. BANG, BANG, BANG.)

FLO "Open Udder End."

(They laugh. SPRINKLE, SPRINKLE, SPRINKLE. PFFFLLL. BANG, BANG, BANG. EDNA sighs. FLO sighs.)

EDNA In Polish, I mean.

FLO *Oh* sure.

(PFFFLLL. Then EDNA carries the "whipped cream can" back to the "refrigerator," while FLO SPRINKLES, then BANG, BANG, BANG. EDNA opens the "refrigerator door" and the "refrigerator" light shines on her a moment, then goes out.)

EDNA He says to me, Mrs. Pavletski, I hope yer not offended. I says to um, Fodder, when yer Polish—what can offend you?

FLO When my Stosh tried to burn a wasps' nest outta the garotch an burnt da garotch down—that was a Polish joke. *(Sighs.)*

EDNA *(Sighs.)* Well, I guess we got a minute.

FLO I guess we'r done till da funeral gets back.

(The wail behind them closes up. They circle the "table," FLO one way, EDNA the other, pointing to things to make sure they're ready. Then)

FLO Yeah, I guess we'r ready.

(Each pulls out a "chair" we don't see on one side of the table. Just as the women are about to sit down on nothing, two STAGEHANDS run in with chairs and hold them for the women, who sit down with weary sighs, not acknowledging the presence of the STAGEHANDS.)

EDNA Flo, you always make da best apple slices. Wher's da
forks . . .

(She reaches for a fork we don't see, and a STAGEHAND *produces one,*
holding it out, and she takes it without acknowledging the STAGEHAND.*)*

FLO Well, Edna, you make da best angel food. Wher's da forks . . .

*(*FLO *reaches for a fork we don't see, and the other* STAGEHAND *hands her*
one. They both reach their forks to plates that aren't there, and two other
STAGEHANDS *run in with plates of dessert. Without acknowledging the*
STAGEHANDS *the women each take a small piece.)*

EDNA Oll just take a small one.

FLO Oll just take a little piece, dey'll never notice.

EDNA Flo.

FLO Look at dat. Just delicious . . .

EDNA Flo.

FLO Odda know how ya do it, Ed.

EDNA Flo, when I die, will ya do my funeral breakfast?

(Pause.)

FLO Sure I will, Ed.

EDNA Will you make yer apple slices?

FLO Sure, Ed.

EDNA An will ya make sure da choir don't sing dat damn song?

FLO Sure I will, Ed.

EDNA Thank you, Flo.

FLO An if I go first, will you do my funeral breakfast?

EDNA You know I will, Flo. I could make duck-blood soup.

FLO Don't bodder with da duck blood. Angel food is fine.

(She takes EDNA's *hand and squeezes it, holding on to it. A radiant cone*
of light bathes the two women, and two doves appear, one over each of their
heads. Without surprise) Edna, ya know ya got a dove over yer head?

EDNA *(Without surprise)* Ya know ya got one, too, Flo?

FLO Yeah, well.

EDNA Yeah, well.

(They reach for another dessert, and a STAGEHAND *steps in with a bowl heaped with fruit for them to take. Each woman takes an apple and polishes it on her dress.)*

FLO "Open Udder End."

EDNA "Open Udder End . . ." 'At's—real—good.

(They laugh gently. EDNA *and* FLO *sigh deeply, in chorus. The lights fade.)*

The Final Interrogation of Ceauşescu's Dog

2000 >WARREN LEIGHT

ORIGINAL EST PRODUCTION

DIRECTOR Jack Hofsiss
SET DESIGNER Carlo Adinolfi
COSTUME DESIGNER Bruce Goodrich
SOUND Robert Gould
PROPS Laura Raynor
PRODUCTION STAGE MANAGER Jim Ring
STAGE MANAGER James Carringer

The cast was as follows:
MAN Ean Sheehy
DOG Alexander R. Scott

This play was originally produced in workshop by All Seasons Theatre Company. (Artistic Director, John McCormach.)

CHARACTERS

MAN

DOG

PLACE

Bucharest

TIME

New Year's Eve, 1989

A small interrogation room. A MAN *paces, smokes cigarettes. A* DOG *sits on a chair. The* MAN *is thin and exhausted. He wears a threadbare winter coat. The* DOG *displays a regal bearing and wears a warmer coat. Both speak in a Romanian accent, but the* DOG's *accent is of a higher class. Throughout the interrogation, the* DOG *very seldom makes eye contact with the* MAN *and never loses his composure.*

MAN The people believe you are beyond reform. Some want you to suffer; others, to die right away. Because ours is now a just and fair system, you are entitled to make a statement. What do you have to say for yourself?

DOG I am Ceaușescu's dog. His daughter's dog, actually, but she is rather unstable. Even though he gave me to her, I have always considered him to be my true master.

MAN You know that your master was a cruel and ruthless tyrant who brought misery to his people and shame to his nation?

DOG I am dog of Ceaușescu, and my relationship to him is simple relationship of dog to master.

MAN You do acknowledge that your master was a tyrant?

DOG No. The wife can be a bit stern, I will say that. And the daughter, as I say, has many moods. But I am my master's pride and joy and I've known nothing but love and affection from him.

MAN You are talking about the most reviled despot in our nation's history. Do you understand that anyone still loyal to him is subject to the death penalty?

DOG Listen, where is my master? He will straighten this whole thing out, and you will be sorry. Let me tell you.

MAN Your master is dead. He was shot . . . like a dog. In the courtyard, as he tried to flee the people's wrath on Christmas Day.

DOG He will not be happy when he hears how you have treated me.

MAN He is not coming back. He has gone straight to hell, where he will burn for all time.

DOG He travels often, you know. Just last month he was in Iran. They love him everywhere he goes. He told me so.

MAN He was shot dead. He is not coming back.

DOG I see.

MAN Do you?

DOG No. I am simple dog.

MAN The people believe you are beyond reform.

DOG I am simple doggie.

MAN But you lived on imported meat. While our people were starving, you ate the finest veal.

DOG Sometimes lamb or steak.

MAN While people starved.

DOG I did not see any people starving.

MAN You didn't?

DOG The people at the palace were all well fed. They ate anything I left over. Often they even pinched some for themselves—but what can you do—servants.

MAN I have heard they weighed your veal on a scale of gold.

DOG Yes, and I will tell you the truth, that was not done for my benefit. The gold, I always felt, left a slight metallic taste. I believe this all came about so that the servants would not pinch from my supper.

MAN While our people lacked basic medical care, you were given drugs and vitamins flown in from Prague.

DOG I have allergies.

MAN You were bathed daily in glacier water.

DOG I hated the baths. Again, because of my allergies, I—

MAN How did you feel about the sacrifices the people were making? The suffering they endured while you were pampered.

DOG The people always loved me. The servants were especially kind to me. Once . . . once, I was mistreated, but that did not happen again.

MAN Yes, you bit the hand of Salvo, while he was feeding you. He slapped you, and then because he slapped you, he was put to death. Is that correct?

DOG I was not slapped again by him.

MAN It's true, then, that you bit the hand that fed you?

DOG Sure.

MAN Why?

DOG It tastes good.

MAN *(Restrains himself.)* Weren't you aware that it might cause suffering?

DOG I did not suffer.

MAN But the man whose hand you bit—

DOG I don't understand.

MAN You bit the man's hand.

DOG Yes. Of course.

MAN He was trying to feed you?

DOG Yes. Yes. But we've been over this.

MAN Weren't you aware it might cause suffering?

DOG I did not suffer.

MAN But the man whose hand you bit . . .

DOG Yes?

MAN Did you not, for one second, think about him his hand, the pain you—

(DOG stares at the MAN's hand, which is close to the DOG's mouth.)

DOG His hand was here. If he did not want me to bite it, he should not have placed it so near my teeth. Listen, where is my master, he will straighten this out.

MAN Your master is dead!

DOG You don't know him.

MAN *(Very frustrated)* The interrogation cannot end until . . . *(Calms himself again.)* In your house, you had your own Oriental rug.

DOG It was Bokhara.

MAN A Bokhara?

DOG Yes. Again, this was not my choice. I liked the *feel* of it, but its taste was nothing to get excited about.

MAN *(Outraged)* And this rug was red, was it not? The same color as the blood shed by our people under the hand of your master?

DOG Again, I loved the feel of it, but the color, that was for them. I do not see color, you know. I am simple dog.

MAN You are a simple dog?

DOG Yes.

MAN Then fetch. *(He throws his hat on the ground.)*

DOG Pardon.

MAN Fetch this, simple doggie. Come on! Fetch, little doggie.

(The MAN *now drops to his knees. He lifts the hat up and down, to try to capture the* DOG's *attention. The* DOG, *as always, couldn't care less.)*

DOG You are joking.

MAN Jump up. Jump! Go on. Jump. Jump. You are simple dog, then fetch. Fetch. Come on!

(The MAN *seems to have completely lost it now. He is on all fours, by the* DOG's *chair. The* DOG *looks at him with utter disdain.)*

DOG Are you out of your mind? Do you know who my master is?

MAN Your master is dead.

DOG You do not know him.

MAN *(Crying now)* He is not coming back.

DOG Really, well, in that case, I will just sit right here and wait for him to come back. You may go now. When I want something, I will let you know.

(The MAN, *broken, sits by the* DOG's *chair. The* DOG *seems unmoved. After a while, he disdainfully reaches out to pat the* MAN *on the head. Then decides against it, as the lights fade to black.)*

Madmen

2000 › ROMULUS LINNEY

ORIGINAL PRODUCTION

DIRECTOR Eileen Myers
SET DESIGNER Warren Karp
COSTUME DESIGNER Amela Baksic
SOUND Beatrice Terry
PROPS Cynthia Franks
PRODUCTION STAGE MANAGER John Thornberry
STAGE MANAGER Diane Healy

The cast was as follows:
FATHER ABBOT ESCOBEDO DE LA AIXA Peter Maloney
MADMAN Ross Gibby

CHARACTERS

ESCOBEDO DE LA AIXA Abbot of Ripal; he is old and not well
MADMAN in his early thirties, handsome and sensitive

PLACE

A garden of the Abbey of Ripal, Spain

TIME

1485

NOTE

Madmen is Part Three of a play entitled *Spain* (Dramatists Play
Service, 1994). In Part One, Tomas de Torquemada, Inquisitor
General, presides over a trial that becomes farcical, due to the
humane actions of the abbot of a monastery, who began some early
treatments of the insane and was tolerant of sexual behavior.
Torquemada condemns all concerned, has them burned at the stake,
and has the remains of the now dead abbot dug up and thrown into
the gutter. In Part Two, a New York psychiatrist of Spanish
descent, Dr. Anna Rey, is researching the life of the forgotten abbot
to fight her own mental instability and suicidal impulses. A very
young man comes to see her. Beneath his youth, innocence, and
desperation she uncovers the paranoid schizophrenia from which he
suffers. In a hallucination of her own, the long dead abbot speaks to
her and she renews her dedication to the mentally ill. She commits
the young man to a hospital, but dedicates herself personally to his
care. Part Three returns to Spain, ten years before the play began,
to a garden of the Abbey of Ripal, where the abbot of a monastery
began treatment of madmen.

Two stone benches in a garden of the Abbey of Ripal. Birds singing.
Enter MADMAN *and* ESCOBEDO DE LA AIXA. *Both are simply dressed:*
ESCOBEDO DE LA AIXA *in a brown monk's robe, with a large wooden cross*
around his neck; the MADMAN *in a similar but ragged and soiled robe.*
The MADMAN *enters first, striding, then stands arms crossed, waiting*
fiercely. ESCOBEDO DE LA AIXA *enters after him, slowly.*

MADMAN Letter of conduct?

AIXA Here. (*He holds it up.*)

MADMAN Prove it.

AIXA How?

MADMAN That's up to you.

AIXA Very well. (*He holds out a stained and torn piece of parchment.*) If
I read it, will you believe it?

MADMAN I may.

AIXA (*Reading*) "Father Abbot Escobedo de la Aixa, Abbey of Ripal:
Holy Father: For the past year, a person who claims himself to
be Father Abbot, that is, you, together with a number of men
saying they are monks from your abbey, have come to this
asylum. Inmates are released into their custody. One monk to
one inmate. They spend time together, walking to the abbey and
back. One very old monk spends time with me. He says that he
is you. We walk and talk in what he says is a garden of the
abbey, which, while very pleasant, could be another place
entirely. This same old man says he will come again this week.
If you are truly this old man, bring this letter with you so I will
know who you are." Unsigned. Well?

MADMAN Give me the letter. (AIXA *hands it to him.*) Yes. There is
my mud stain in the corner.

AIXA You stained it in the upper corner, too. See?

MADMAN Right or left?

AIXA Left.

MADMAN Then you must be Father Abbot.

AIXA You have proved it.

MADMAN Hm. I was a student of divine logic before I knew I was God. *(He thinks a moment, sits on a bench.)* Now I wrestle with evil, not by destroying others, but by destroying myself. Do you see that?

AIXA I get a glimpse of it.

MADMAN You want to joke with me?

AIXA To understand things.

MADMAN Your worship.

AIXA Your worship.

MADMAN I have no sacred name. That is a pitiful superstition which my arrival on earth has superseded. Mysterious gods assuming powers only when a secret name is uttered? That's absurd. The folly of corrupted and obsessed theologians set on fire by numbers. Do you know why theologians are set on fire by numbers?

AIXA No, your worship.

MADMAN They can't face me. I make them feel tender, ravishing, beautiful, and exalted things, more like music than the sterile ideas they cherish. They can't stand it. They can't give themselves to anything. Let alone me. So they hide behind exploded formulas and columns of faceless numbers.

AIXA Fascinating.

MADMAN My love for them is what they can't bear. Can you understand *that*?

AIXA I am trying. Your worship.

MADMAN I live in a verminous cell, beaten and scorned. Why? To protect mankind from myself. I would blind your pig-faced fools who make up so much of the world. They deserve to have all their terrible brains knocked out. Their eyes burned out. Their cocks and their balls torn from their groins, cooked over a fire, and eaten by their own children. But I am a God of Love and I don't do things like that. I must help them understand each other and stop hurting each other so much. I have a new idea about that. *(Pause. Listens.)* Oh! Rua.

AIXA A change of subject.

MADMAN My favorite bird.

AIXA Mine, too.

MADMAN Really? They sound like this: "Ru-ah! Ru-ah!"

AIXA Children love them.

MADMAN I did.

AIXA So did I.

MADMAN They were like I was inside.

AIXA Calling out.

MADMAN "Ru-ah! Ru-ah!" Sometimes they get into the asylum. They fly about, frightened. Sometimes they hit the walls and fall down. I pick them up and tell them it will be all right. I will set them free, into the blue sky. They will fly into the sunshine, my beautiful, beautiful white light.

AIXA You let them go.

MADMAN Whenever I can.

AIXA When I was a boy, I whistled to them.

MADMAN "Ru-ah! Ru-ah!" *(AIXA whistles.)* No, they trill the *r*. Like this.

(They both whistle, stop, and listen. The birds respond: "Ru-ah! Ru-ah!")

AIXA Modest creatures. No color. Simple, brown, and small. But their song calls to us.

(Birds sing: "Ru-ah. Ru-ah." MADMAN calls back to them. AIXA whistles. Pause.)

MADMAN Pig-faced fools!

AIXA How could we forget?

MADMAN My new idea. How to make them stop hurting each other and us. Do you want to hear it?

AIXA I want to listen to you.

MADMAN No, you don't. You're an old fox.

AIXA Not a bear or a tiger?

MADMAN Fox. You want me to laugh.

AIXA Laughter is good for you.

MADMAN I can laugh with you.

AIXA How does it feel to laugh?

MADMAN Strange, then good. Then strange again. I may die for everybody. Good and bad alike. Is that funny? I will take everything upon myself. You aren't laughing.

AIXA I will when I can.

MADMAN God sheds his blood for pig-faced fools. Then they will be ashamed and stop their dreadful hatreds and persecutions. Then the world will be gentle and kind and there will be peace, in gardens like this one. Where everybody can laugh.

AIXA That would be a very good thing.

MADMAN That's my idea.

AIXA Do you have others?

MADMAN Yes.

AIXA Please.

MADMAN I'll do nothing. Just live out my life with vermin and lunatics. Never be discovered by anybody. Deny pig-faced fools my presence at all. Doing nothing can be very powerful. Understand *that*?

AIXA Yes, your worship.

MADMAN I'm still not sure you're who you say you are.

AIXA My letter of conduct.

MADMAN Well, that's true.

AIXA You wrote it.

MADMAN So I did.

(Pause.)

AIXA Talk to me.

MADMAN Madmen need friends.

AIXA Yes.

MADMAN You do understand that.

AIXA I do.

MADMAN The monks. With us. Your idea?

AIXA I learned it from others.

MADMAN Who?

AIXA Heathen Moors. They call you holy.

MADMAN Does it make you feel holy to agree with heathen Moors?

AIXA Well—

MADMAN Does it makes you feel like God?

AIXA No!

MADMAN Yes, it does!

AIXA *(Laughing)* Well, sometimes.

MADMAN *(Laughing)* You see?

AIXA *(Laughing)* Yes!

MADMAN *(Laughing)* You are God in your way. I am God in mine.

AIXA That is very well put.

MADMAN Thank you. *(Pause. They move about.)* A beautiful day!

AIXA I am glad you like it. You didn't use to.

MADMAN I was afraid of you.

AIXA Not anymore.

MADMAN You might see to a little weeding over there. Those
hedges need tending.

AIXA Some things come first.

MADMAN Like what?

AIXA Prayer.

MADMAN To me?

AIXA To our Lord Jesus Christ.

MADMAN That's me.

AIXA Ah.

MADMAN I won't argue about it.

AIXA Neither will I.

MADMAN Fragrance. Peace. Rua birds.

(Pause.)

AIXA All is well. *(Pause. The* MADMAN *breathes in the air. Then he suddenly bends over and hides his face in his hands.)* What's the matter?

MADMAN Nothing!

AIXA You can tell me.

MADMAN No, I can't.

AIXA If you want to, you can.

MADMAN You couldn't bear it!

AIXA I could try.

MADMAN So many things go wrong.

AIXA Like what?

MADMAN Those I love betray me.

AIXA That must hurt.

MADMAN They do it because I'm dirt.

AIXA Why do you say that?

MADMAN I am dirt and God is dirt.

AIXA Is that really what you mean?

MADMAN Yes!

AIXA Maybe not.

MADMAN What else?

AIXA Something—underneath the dirt.

MADMAN I live with madmen. What's underneath them?

AIXA I don't know.

MADMAN When I was a theology student, I learned to think. So I think about that now.

AIXA You think very well.

MADMAN I am logic itself!

AIXA You work very hard at it.

MADMAN Exactly.

AIXA Exactly.

MADMAN Then why am I in an asylum?

AIXA Perhaps you make an illogical assumption, then become so logical about it.

MADMAN Example?

AIXA You give me one.

MADMAN I am God. What logically follows is madness? Is that what you mean?

AIXA Yes.

MADMAN When someone is not who they say they are and want to hurt me and I hit them to keep them from hurting me?

AIXA Or send them letters of conduct, to prove they won't hurt you, yes.

MADMAN But sometimes people do hurt people.

AIXA That is true.

MADMAN They burn them at the stake.

AIXA Sometimes.

MADMAN I am right to be afraid.

AIXA Sometimes.

MADMAN Of the Inquisition now.

AIXA Possibly.

MADMAN What else is underneath dirt?

AIXA You tell me.

MADMAN Indifference. I don't pray enough?

AIXA I didn't say that.

MADMAN It's what you mean! How many prayers today! How many tomorrow! Collecting prayers! Numbers again! Corrupt and obsessed theologians, set on fire by numbers! You are like all the rest!

AIXA Forget anything I said.

(Pause.)

MADMAN Why do you care about me?

AIXA You are God's, as I am.

MADMAN *(Laughing)* Oh, really. Anything else? *(Pause.)* Please.

AIXA Well, you try so hard.

MADMAN To do what?

AIXA To be good. To do right. To think logically. You can't, because you can't be God, but you are trying. I admire you.

MADMAN I can't be God?

AIXA No.

MADMAN You don't believe I am Jesus Christ on earth?

AIXA No.

MADMAN Who am I, then?

AIXA You are a man who would be God, if he could, and save the world.

MADMAN Hm. *(Pause.)* I know this is the last time we will see each other. *(Pause.)* That's what's really bothering me. *(Pause.)* Underneath everything. *(Pause.)* You're leaving me. Did you hear me?

AIXA Yes.

MADMAN I listen to walls.

AIXA I believe you.

MADMAN They talk.

AIXA I believe you.

MADMAN Will I ever see you again?

AIXA Perhaps not.

MADMAN Will you ever believe I am God?

AIXA No. But like God, you see my heart. If I am false, you know it. If I am truthful, you know it.

MADMAN Madmen are like that. So is God.

AIXA If I want to hurt you, you know it.

MADMAN Instantly.

AIXA We've been good friends.

MADMAN Yes.

AIXA You know I wouldn't hurt you.

MADMAN Yes.

AIXA You wouldn't talk to me at first. You do now.

MADMAN Your heart is pure.

AIXA Thank you.

MADMAN There is a new Inquisitor General. Does he live in his Burning Mountain?

AIXA That's just his name. Torquemada.

MADMAN Does Torquemada make assumptions and proceed logically?

AIXA Yes.

MADMAN Like madmen.

AIXA Yes.

MADMAN Does the fire hurt?

AIXA For a while.

MADMAN He can say we are heretics, talking to Satan.

AIXA Let us hope not.

MADMAN But he does!

AIXA Yes, he does.

MADMAN It's logical.

AIXA To him.

MADMAN God means devil means torture means fire?

AIXA That is the way some minds work.

MADMAN We can't laugh about that, can we?

AIXA No!

MADMAN These visits will stop?

AIXA After today.

MADMAN Burning Mountain.

AIXA I can't talk about this.

MADMAN It's all right. Madmen understand inquisitions.

AIXA Do you?

MADMAN Inquisitors think they know who is mad and who isn't.

AIXA Yes.

MADMAN Who belongs to the devil and who doesn't.

AIXA Yes.

MADMAN Do you think I belong to the devil?

AIXA No!

MADMAN What will happen to me?

AIXA You will be loved by God, who created you.

MADMAN In the fire, can I think of this garden?

AIXA Yes!!!

MADMAN What's the matter?

AIXA I'm sorry!

MADMAN You're crying.

AIXA I'm all right now. Where were we?

MADMAN I know that look. I was a student. That's theological cramps. We got them when we realized nothing about God made any sense. Will Burning Mountain burn you, too?

AIXA I don't care if he does.

MADMAN Don't be discouraged. If *you* get discouraged, what will happen to *me*?

AIXA To destroy it all! A year ago, a raving lunatic asylum! Then, by just walking about, saying nothing, listening, passing no judgments, we calmed you! We helped you!

MADMAN Luis Aceves Guilman cut his throat. But he was crazy. Two others died, but they were sick.

AIXA But the rest? You! Calm. Tranquil. Beginning, if not to trust exactly, at least to begin—to try—to believe—you could *perhaps* trust someone. Someday. We did that together, you and I.

MADMAN And now?

AIXA Torquemada.

MADMAN Burning Mountain.

AIXA Yes.

MADMAN A theologian making logic.

AIXA Yes.

MADMAN He will burn us both.

AIXA Ah!

MADMAN Don't cry! (*He embraces* AIXA. AIXA *embraces the* MADMAN.) It will be all right, someday. I will be burned, but you are so old, maybe you will die first. Burning will hurt me for a little while, but then I will go away, into a beautiful white place that will be eternal. I will wait for you in a great garden of light and rest. You will come soon, because you are unhappy now and sick trying to be sensible and do good things for others. I will be waiting for you and I won't judge you, either. I'll just say hello.

(AIXA *is trying not to weep.*)

AIXA Will you, your worship?

MADMAN I promise. When the Burning Mountain has betrayed us long enough, and the world lies in ashes, we must begin our life all over again. Someone somewhere will remember you, that you lived in Spain and loved madmen. That will be good. Believe in me.

(AIXA *weeps.*)

AIXA I do!

MADMAN Have faith.

AIXA I will!

MADMAN The soul, like a bird, will fly into the white light, with music playing of such tender, such ravishing beauty, that we will both be exalted. I will take you into my arms and hold you fast, in heaven above.

(*The* MADMAN *holds* AIXA *in his arms. Birds sing. Lights fade.*)

Accident

2000

>PETER MALONEY

ORIGINAL PRODUCTION

DIRECTOR Beatrice Terry
SET DESIGNER Chris Jones
COSTUME DESIGNER Julie Doyle
SOUND Beatrice Terry
PROPS Laura Raynor
PRODUCTION STAGE MANAGER Jim Ring
STAGE MANAGER Jeannine L. Jones
SPECIAL EFFECTS Fred Buccholz

The cast was as follows:
PETER Peter Maloney
THE SHADOW Griffith Maloney
VOICES Bronwyn Maloney and Mark Mitton

CHARACTERS

PETER
THE SHADOW
VOICES — BRONWYN, GRIFFITH, X-RAY TECHNICIAN, INTERNS, REGIS

TIME

The present

Onstage, a table six feet long and a chair with arms. On the floor in front of the table lies a doll-like figure of a man, three-quarter size, facedown, outlined in chalk.

PETER enters quickly, dragging behind him a large black plastic bag full of something bulky and heavy and carrying a long object wrapped in a ratty old comforter. He walks right down to the audience.

PETER Hey, did I tell you about my accident? Jeez, you won't believe this. I broke my arm. I broke it right off at the shoulder. *(He sets the long object on the table, the black bag on the chair.)* I've got Death in this bag. Before I fell, there were certain premonitions, certain signs. I'm walking my daughter home from school one day when she suddenly turns and asks me:

BRONWYN *(Voice-over)* "Dad, how come all my friends think you're my grandfather?"

PETER This is what is called the "shock of recognition." Bronwyn is eight. I'm fifty-eight. I am half a century older than my daughter. *(Music. Something with a hip-hop beat, maybe a number by the Bloodhound Gang.)* What?! What?!

(THE SHADOW enters the space, pushing a platform on wheels on which is mounted a clothing rack made of pipe. It's the kind of rack you see being

pushed around the garment district. From the rack hang hooks and wires of various lengths. THE SHADOW *is six feet tall and clothed entirely in black; a black hood obscures his face, he wears black gloves from which the thumbs have been removed, only his white thumbs are visible. He is on black roller blades.* PETER *is alarmed at* THE SHADOW'S *presence, but continues talking.)*

PETER My son, Griffith, is another story altogether. He had just turned thirteen and had only recently got his hair cut, for the first time since he was three years old. For years he was the only boy in his school with long hair, hair halfway down his back, refusing to cut it, like some follower of Shiva. When he was little, old ladies, most of the time thinking he was a girl child, would ask him, "Wherever did you get such beautiful red hair?" Griff would smile up from his stroller, point to my bald head, and say, "I got it from my dad." And he would laugh. But now that he's a teenager, he says, "Dad, I'm getting tired of all these cross-gender jokes." I say, "Well, there's an easy way out of that, just cut your hair.' "But my hair is me, my hair is who I am." "Maybe," I say. He finally cut it off. I've got it now.

(He takes a braid of red hair from his pocket, looks at it, rubs his head. THE SHADOW, *making a loop around the table, snatches the braid out of* PETER's *hand, skates back up, and hangs the braid from the rack.)*

My son has always been the sweetest, kindest, most compassionate boy, but lately . . . Soon after Bronwyn's question, Griff comes to me and asks:

GRIFF *(Voice-over)* "Dad, do you know of any occult supply houses in the neighborhood?"

PETER And he hands me a crumpled piece of paper, saying, "If you come across one, here are some things I *need*. I'll pay you back, okay?" *(He takes a piece of crumpled paper from a pocket.)* These are the things he asked me to get: thyme oil, clove oil, sage oil,

eight-foot leather strings, six python vertebrae, eight python
ribs, four ostrich neck vertebrae, a bison incisor, a shark tooth,
an apache tear, a monkey jawbone. What is happening to my
son?

(THE SHADOW *skates past, takes the paper from* PETER's *hand, and hangs
it from a clip on the rack.*)

Look at this!

(*He goes up to the table and unwraps the long object. It is a rough wooden
staff made from a thick tree branch, and it has been decorated with all of
the animal bones listed above, some of which hang from leather thongs.*)

I took this from his room. Phew! It stinks. Of thyme and clove
and sage and sweat. What is it? A walking stick? My son never
walks! Most of the time he's flat on his back, video-game
controller balanced on his belly, never walking, no. A shaman's
stick, a magic staff, like Prospero's?

(THE SHADOW *skates down, takes the staff, puts it on the wheeled rack
upstage.* PETER *hangs the comforter on the rack.*)

You could kill someone with that! We've always been so close,
my son and I, but now . . . And I decide we need to do
something together, father and son, to ensure that we remain
friends, or at least don't become enemies. We need to bond . . .
Hey, we can exercise together! It was Griff's idea to buy roller
blades.

(THE SHADOW *opens the black bag.*)

I didn't mind spending the money. And the roller blades were
on sale. I got 'em for fifty bucks. I've got the receipt right
here . . .

(*He takes the receipt from his shirt pocket and reads.*)

Fifty-four dollars and twelve cents, to be exact.

(THE SHADOW *skates down, takes the receipt. Music.* PETER *sits on the
table.*)

Now, I used to skate, I was a good skater. In my hometown, when the creek froze, you could skate from above the falls all the way to North Bloomfield, the next town over.

(THE SHADOW *takes an oil portrait of* PETER, *age six, from the bag, sets it on the table.*)

I told Griff about roller-skating in front of the Methodist church, across the street from Tommy Mamoone's father's barbershop, where the really smooth sidewalk was. I was telling him about the metal keys Tommy and I used to tighten our skates onto our shoes . . .

(THE SHADOW *pulls an in-line skate from the bag, hands it to* PETER.)

All the while I'm flipping closed the high-impact plastic buckles on my new Spiritblades, featuring ABT, that's Active Brake Technology (a registered trademark of Rollerblade, Inc.).

(THE SHADOW *takes skate and portrait, hangs them from the rack.*)

Now, put Griff on a pair of blades and he is *unbelievably* graceful. And as for me, well, they say that once you learn to skate, like typing or driving a car, you never forget.

(*He stands. The music becomes ominous.*)

It was a beautiful day, September 4, the Friday of Labor Day weekend. The city was empty of people. At 8:30 a.m. the only sounds were those of the birds in the trees and the strokes of our wheels on the tiles surrounding Central Park's newly refurbished Great Lawn.

(*Birdsong, then the sound of plastic wheels on the tiles is heard as* PETER *"skates." He gets more red-faced and out of breath with every stride. He stands, recovers.*)

We had just skated four miles and were headed home. Now, between the reservoir and Central Park West, two macadam paths branch off from the park drive. One comes out at West Eighty-sixth Street, the other angles up to Ninety-first. I say to

Griff, "Let's go the short way home." But he says— And I must tell you, I have been working since November on a production of *Oedipus Rex*, and if you remember, in Sophocles' play Oedipus kills his father, Laius, King of Thebes, at a place *where three roads meet*! And furthermore, if you remember, he kills him with a blow of his *staff*! Griff says, "No, let's go the long way home." It turned out to be a very long way home indeed.

The grade was not a particularly steep one, but what we couldn't see, at the bottom of the slope, was a pile of acorns, left there by a squirrel who no doubt knew that winter was a-comin'-in. Give me a hand with this, will you?

*(*PETER, *wearing a helmet, and* THE SHADOW *pick up the doll, which is dressed exactly like* PETER, *with small roller blades on its feet, bring it to the table, and, like Bunraku puppeteers, they manipulate the doll as* PETER *speaks.)*

So, the nuts get in my wheels, sending me wobbling to the left. My wheels hit the stone edging the path, which stops them dead, but I keep going, up and forward, and, afraid I'll break both wrists, I turn in midair . . .

(They lift the puppet's head. It wears PETER*'s face, frozen in an expression of fright and horror.)*

And land on my right shoulder on the hard-packed earth.

(They drop the puppet on the floor. PETER *screams once, grimaces exactly as the puppet is grimacing, and the sound of the scream is heard echoing along with the sound of* GRIFF *laughing.* PETER *points up to where the sound is coming from.)*

Griff was right behind me, and he laughed out loud, of course, to see Dad fall so funny. I say "of course," but the question lingers: Was it *inevitable* that he should laugh? Did I laugh when I saw my own father fall? Off the ladder he'd foolishly balanced on a picnic table? The table tipping, followed by the ladder, then by my father, from the second story of our house? And did I laugh? *I don't think so.* But now Griff's dad is writhing in the dirt and the dog shit, screaming curses and obscenities into the September air.

(GRIFF'S *laugh is heard again.*)

Griff finally stops laughing and runs home to get Jocasta . . . uh, Kristin . . . his mom, who soon arrives with a policewoman, who radios for an ambulance. We wait there for an hour, me moaning all the while and gathering acorns.

(*He takes acorns from his pocket, passes them from hand to hand.*)

These are the acorns that got in my wheels. I've kept them, as evidence. I have the squirrel, too. Not with me. He's at the taxidermist's, being stuffed.

(THE SHADOW *skates down with a Ziploc bag, collects nuts from* PETER, *hangs up the bag. The sound of an ambulance is heard.* PETER *picks up the puppet.* THE SHADOW *skates by and takes it from* PETER, *hangs it on the rack.*)

The ambulance finally arrives, and the driver asks, "Uptown or downtown?" and we, don't ask me why, say, "Down," which word perfectly describes the direction my life is to take in the immediate future.

(*He sits on the table.*)

We sit on a bench in the back of the ambulance. I'm trying to hold my shoulder together while the driver hits every pothole on Columbus Avenue.

(THE SHADOW *repeatedly lifts, then drops, the right end of the table.*)

"Agggh! Agggh! Agggh!" The driver misses the emergency entrance and has to go around the block, hitting some of the same potholes again. "Agggh! Agggh!" And now the descent into darkness begins. The ambulance doors open. Kristin steps down, helping me with one hand, my roller blades in the other.

The crowd outside the emergency room sees us coming, and interns, ambulance drivers, policemen, firemen, like a modern-day Greek chorus, all sneer in unison, "Oh, another in-line skater!" Try it, all together now, "Oh, another . . ." No, no, with more *derision*, you can do it. "Oh, another in-line skater!" That's it, and that welcome set the tone for my entrance into hospital #1, which I will call the House of Pain.

(*He removes his shirt, under which he wears a hospital gown. He throws the shirt to* THE SHADOW, *who hangs it on the rack.*)

An efficient and kindly nurse gives me a very welcome shot of Demerol. I stand shivering on the cold floor of the X-ray room, waiting for the technician to develop the plate he's just exposed. Suddenly, from the developing room, comes a cry . . .

X-RAY TECHNICIAN (*Voice-over*) Oh my God!!!!

(THE SHADOW *takes an X-ray from the black bag, hands it to* PETER.)

PETER The X-ray revealed that I had broken the ball at the top of my right humerus bone into three large pieces and a number of smaller fragments. I had broken the humerus itself—that's this bone here—*off* the ball completely. I'm sitting in a wheelchair, and two interns are standing on either side of me, passing my X-ray back and forth over my head. This is what I hear:

(THE SHADOW *stands behind* PETER *and passes the X-ray from his right to his left hand over* PETER'*s head.*)

INTERN #1 (*Voice-over*) I've never seen one as bad as this.

INTERN #2 (*Voice-over*) Yeah, I've got no idea how he's going to fix this one!

(THE SHADOW *takes the X-ray and hangs it up.*)

PETER Well, *however* he fixed it, whoever *he* turned out to be, we just wanted him to fix it right away. But now the young doctors are saying, "No, no, with an injury like this, there's no rush. In cases like these, sometimes it's not even necessary to *have* surgery." So they put my arm in a sling, tape the sling to my chest, give me a prescription for pain pills, and send me home for five days! Now, all this happened on Friday morning, and I can't see this surgeon till *Tuesday*. Look, I've got the admitting form right here . . .

(He takes the admitting form from a pocket, goes into the audience, and shows individuals the form.)

See? Tuesday! Tuesday! It's okay, it's been a year and a half, I'm over this . . .

(THE SHADOW takes the form, PETER sits on the table.)

So, I'm home in bed, but I can't sleep, and I am there for five days in the Indian-summer heat, and inside the tape and the sling my arm is starting to itch.

(THE SHADOW skates down, a large sponge in his hand. He presses the sponge against PETER's upper arm, painting it bright purple.)

I look down and see a purple bloom . . . the fungal infection candida. I'd had it once before, and it takes *forever* to get rid of it. I see it. Kristin sees it. My kids see it. You can see it! But the surgeon doesn't see it when I finally arrive at his office on *Tuesday* afternoon, because he never looks at me! He looks at my X-rays, but not at me.

Maybe I should have been more suspicious of this guy from the beginning. This is what he had hanging in his office.

(THE SHADOW has taken up his staff. He and PETER approach the bag. PETER opens the mouth of the bag, and THE SHADOW puts the end of the staff inside. Music. Slowly a nearly life-size skeleton rises from the bag. It is supported on the staff and now appears to be standing on the table. THE SHADOW as puppeteer manipulates the skeleton so that it sits on PETER's right knee, puts its left arm across PETER's shoulders, turns its head to look at PETER.)

For those of you who couldn't see the X-ray clearly enough, this is what my broken bone looked like.

(PETER *reaches up and breaks the skeleton's right arm off the ball at the top of the humerus. He holds up the jagged edge of the broken bone, the forearm and hand bones dangling.* THE SHADOW *hangs the skeleton from the rack.* PETER *tosses the bones to* THE SHADOW.)

So, the surgeon looks at my X-rays and says, "I can fix this. How about tomorrow, 6 p.m.?" "Okay," I say, "let's do it." I check into the hospital the next morning, and at six o'clock that evening I am placed on a gurney and rolled down to the operating room. The surgeon is late, but he finally arrives, and they put me under. When I wake up, I turn my head to see that my arm . . . *hasn't been operated on*! I've been put under general anesthesia and *nothing has been done*! The surgeon passes by. "What's up, Doc?" I ask. "I couldn't operate," he says. "You've got an infection, it might be staph." "I know I've got an infection, and it's not staph, it's a fungal infection. It's called candida, and you treat it with a cream called Nizoral and a pink pill the name of which I can't remember." "Oh," he says, and he walks away. They take me back up to my room, but before they do . . . they have to immobilize my arm again. And apparently this huge, famous hospital doesn't have a proper brace in stock, so somebody cuts up a foam-rubber mattress . . .

(THE SHADOW *pulls a homemade brace from the bag.* PETER *takes it, shows it to the audience.*)

. . . glues the pieces together with Krazy Glue and attaches a thin strap to the foam with safety pins. I sleep fitfully, because the strap cuts into my neck, "excoriating," I think the medical term for it is, the skin there.

I am awakened the next morning by cries of anguish from the other side of the curtain dividing my room. It's my roommate, Terry, an Irish-Catholic bachelor of indeterminate age, who has just had a hip replacement. "Pete, Pete!" he hollers. "That woman! Whenever she tries to help me out of bed, she hurts me so much!" "Don't let her touch you," I shout back. "Demand another nurse!"

Thinking I had summoned her, a nurse comes running into my room. I take advantage of her presence to ask her what this new bag is, hanging next to my regular IV, and she says, "Oh, that's just the antibiotics, for your infection." "No, no! You don't treat a fungal infection with antibiotics; antibiotics *feed* a fungal infection!" The nurse, looking irritated that a patient has expressed an opinion, leaves the room. Five minutes later she comes running back, says, "I'd better take this down." Uh-huh.

Another day and a night go by, and I realize I haven't seen my son since he stopped laughing at me and ran off to get his mother.

(Sound of laughter, distant, echoing. THE SHADOW *takes from the bag a child's painting, tempera on paper. He hands it to* PETER.*)*

Griff did this painting when he was in pre-K. Mrs. Chen asked the kids to paint pictures of their families. I said, "Oh, there's Mom, and there's you, and there's me." "No, that's not you, that's Grandmother." "Oh, where am I?" And he points to this . . . *blob* in the far corner of the picture, this . . . I don't know if you can even see this . . . this . . . cockroach, whatever it is . . . You know, the ancient Greeks knew how to read signs. I mean, their priests could look inside a dead bird and predict what was going to happen in the future, and *this* . . . *this* is exactly the kind of thing that drove Laius, King of Thebes, to pierce his young son Oedipus' ankles with iron spikes and leave him exposed to the elements on the slopes of Mount Cithaeron.

*(*THE SHADOW *takes the picture from* PETER, *hangs it up on the rack.)*

I am meditating on this theme when a Catholic priest walks through the curtain and over to my bed. He has just given Terry

Holy Communion and wants to know if there's anything he can do for me. I knew it was time to get out of there.

Kristin didn't need a priest to tell her we'd be better off elsewhere. She'd been calling around to ask advice, and a friend of a friend got us into another hospital.

So, Kristin packs me up, and as we flee my room, Terry thrusts a book into my good hand.

(THE SHADOW *takes a book from the bag, hands it to* PETER.)

"This'll cheer you up," he says. A copy of *Angela's Ashes*, which he has inscribed: "To Peter, I thank God for giving me a roommate so understanding. Peter, I will remember you in my prayers." Well, I am not a religious man, but I mutter a prayer for Terry as we struggle into a cab and speed away from the House of Pain.

We stumble out of the cab and into the *Hospital for Special Surgery*, and it is like . . . walking into heaven after several eons in purgatory. Somebody sees this thing under my arm, says, "What the hell is that?" and "Get this man a proper brace!"

(PETER *takes off the brace, tosses it to* THE SHADOW, *who hangs it on the rack.*)

More X-rays. A young doctor looks at them and right away draws me a picture showing me how they might fix my arm. Then a man comes in, he is so . . . handsome. He has on dark blue hospital scrubs. He is wearing no socks with these expensive loafers. He is incredibly tan, with jet-black hair and a strong, sharp-featured face. He looks like a *god*. He studies my X-rays, leans down, looks directly into my eyes, and says, "You're going to be all right."

(PETER *is overcome with emotion, weeps.* THE SHADOW *skates down with a box of tissues.* PETER *takes one, blows his nose.*)

As it turns out, this guy's specialty is shoulders, and my

problem is a broken arm; he isn't going to have anything to do with me. He sends me upstairs to his colleague, who, he assures me, is one of the greatest orthopedic surgeons, not just in the city, but in the world.

I am laid on a gurney in an empty and pristine room, with a picture window looking out on, and on a level with, the East River. The river is flowing slowly north, and I imagine . . .

(Music. PETER *lies down on the table.)*

I am on a barge in ancient Egypt, floating up the Nile to the next world.

*(*THE SHADOW *takes an inflated yellow ball from the black bag, slowly lifts it like a rising sun, hangs it from a hook above the table.)*

I feel . . . as if I have survived a journey through the perilous night of the underworld and am now, as *The Book of the Dead* would have it, finally "coming forth by day."

*(*THE SHADOW *picks up his staff, sits on the edge of the table, slowly "poles" the "barge.")*

"And may there be made ready for me a seat in the boat of the sun, and may I be received into the presence of Osiris in the land of victory; Osiris, who was treacherously murdered, dismembered, by his brother Seth, he of the red hair and the principle of discord; Osiris, whose sister Isis collected all the limbs of his body and by magical words reconstituted them so he could come to life again. O Ra, may the limbs of *my* body be made new again, bind up my sinews and muscles, and make me to receive the air."

(Music ends. THE SHADOW *retires upstage, taking his staff and the yellow ball with him.* PETER *sits up.)*

My surgeon, Dr. David Helfet, is from Capetown, South Africa. He is handsome, like the other one, but in a different way. His complexion is ruddy, not tan; his hair is silvery gray, not black;

but he, too, looks like a god as he stands over me, points to the purple bloom on my breast, and says, "What's this?" "It's a fungal infection, candida, and you treat it with a cream called Nizoral and a pink pill the name of which I can't remember." "Well," he says, "we'll have to get you some of that cream, won't we? And some of those pink pills."

They put me in a private room, with a view of the river, where I wait for my infection to subside. I am still in pain, but I have painkillers; my spirits are buoyed by calls from relatives, friends, and colleagues. My surgeon comes to see me every day, to see how I'm doing. Imagine that! But my kids still haven't come to visit. I can understand Bronwyn being afraid. She's only eight, and hospitals, as we learned in the House of Pain, can be scary places. But Griff, my Griff, surely he'll come to see me. Unless he simply doesn't want to. Unless he'd rather stay home . . . with his mother.

(A doorbell is heard from off right. THE SHADOW *skates off to answer it.* PETER *goes to the bag, digs inside it, comes out with something made of purple construction paper.)*

On Griff's fourth birthday he brought home this crown he'd made in school. That night, after birthday cake and ice cream, Griff looked at me and said, "Bring me my crown." I picked it up and handed it to him. "No," he said, "bring it to me on a pillow." "What?" "You heard me, slave, bring it to me on a pillow." Well, it *was* his birthday, and he was, after all, just a child, so I brought it to him. "Kneel down, slave," he said. I knelt and offered him the crown. He said since he was King, and since it was his birthday, he planned to sleep upstairs tonight, and added, "With the Queen." "And where am I to sleep? . . . Your Majesty." And here he could not contain his delight any longer; a smile spread like a sunrise across his sweet face. "You," he said, "will sleep down in the cellar, with the other servants." And now I am *truly* down in the cellar. I am tasting the ashes. I'm hurting from the pain and numb from the narcotics, and my scalp is itching 'cause my dermatological shampoo is home in the medicine cabinet and I haven't had a bowel movement in a week, and my libido, which is usually raging, has flown out the window, despite all these nurses, not to mention my beautiful wife, who is home with our son, the adolescent, who is taller than me and whose libido is definitely *not* impaired, who's spending far too much time in the bathroom, who's listening to CDs like "Dirty Deeds Done Dirt Cheap" and "Hooray for Boobies," and who is so smart . . . He's taking a course this summer at Hamilton College, a course in *Shakespeare*. He'll probably study *Hamlet, another* story about mothers and sons . . . He shows the precosity of the destined child, there's no riddle he can't answer: "What walks on four legs in the morning, two legs at noon, and three legs in the evening?"

GRIFF *(Voice-over)* The answer is . . . *man!*

REGIS *(Voice-over)* Is that your final answer?

(PETER *finds a book in the bag, a large picture book of lighthouses.*)

PETER He wants to live in a lighthouse! Talk about transparent! Look at this! What is this guy trying to prove!

(THE SHADOW *skates on with a box wrapped in brown paper.* PETER *opens the package, takes out a stuffed squirrel, smiles. shows it to the audience.* THE SHADOW *skates upstage with the squirrel.*)

The purple bloom eventually fades to pink, and on a Wednesday evening, almost two weeks after the accident, I am wheeled down to the operating room and given local anesthesia.

(THE SHADOW *unhooks the skeleton, lays it on the table, begins to attach the skeleton's arm to its shoulder with adhesive tape.*)

Dr. David Helfet opens me up and performs a perfect open
reduction with internal fixation. In a three-hour operation he
glues together the fragmented head of the humerus, drills holes
in the humerus, holes in the ball, and wires the whole thing
back together.

(He takes another X-ray from the bag.)

I don't know if you can see this, the bright line is the wire,
which is still here in my arm, wound around and through the
bone in a kind of figure-eight design or, if I'm lying down, like
the symbol for infinity.

(He hangs the X-ray on the rack. THE SHADOW *raises the restored skeleton
from the table until it stands upright.)*

And the bones came together, bone to my bone . . . and Dr.
Helfet sewed me up, and that was that.

*(*PETER *holds the black bag open, and* THE SHADOW *lowers the skeleton
into the bag.* PETER *puts the bag on the table.* THE SHADOW *helps* PETER
into his shirt.)

Leaving the Hospital for Special Surgery is a traumatic
experience. I hold on to Kristin's arm with my good left hand,
feeling small, fragile, vulnerable in the face of cars, trucks,
pedestrians, bicycle messengers, and yes, in-line skaters.
Whoooah!

*(*THE SHADOW *skates past* PETER*, almost mowing him down. Scary
music.)*

I get home, and there is Griff, watching some gory movie on the
sci-fi channel.

GRIFF *(Voice-over)* Hey, Dad! Feeling better?

*(*PETER *weakly waves his left hand in greeting.* THE SHADOW *picks up the
yellow ball and throws it to* PETER*, who exercises with it as he speaks.)*

PETER The problem with my shoulder was not so much the broken
bones but the fact that, in the days that I was denied care, scar

tissue had developed and the muscles had atrophied. It took
almost a year of therapy before I could do this:

(He raises his right arm over his head.)

One year and $40,000 later, I can do this, and it only hurts a
little. $40,000. My mother and father bought their house on
Cape Cod for $45,000.

(He tosses the ball to THE SHADOW, *who sets it on the chair.* PETER *takes
the comforter and staff from the rack, comes downstage.)*

So, it's been a year and a half, my bones have knit, my wound
has healed, and for all that, what have I learned? . . . *I don't
know!* A friend says, "Peter, the question is: Why did you fall?"
I don't know.

*(*THE SHADOW *skates past, taking the staff from* PETER, *who drops the
comforter on the floor.)*

I don't know if I want to see my accident as just another
Freudian slip. Another friend, she's a *Jungian*, she says we live
our lives as if we don't *have* bodies, and when we have an
accident like mine, it's a chance for our body to speak to us,
usually for the first time in years. Well, my body spoke to me,
all right. My body *screamed* at me: "What are you doing on roller
blades?! Your son doesn't need you to skate with him. Let him
get a girlfriend to skate with!" Hey, I'm for that. He *needs* a
girlfriend, if only so he'll stop walking down the street with his
arm around his *mother*, like *she's* his girlfriend! Oh, and you'll be
happy to know . . . my libido has returned!

   On Halloween day I take the bus across town to the hospital
to see my physical therapists, Chris and Todd, for the last time.
Climbing the steps to board, I notice two girls sitting in the
seats directly behind the driver. They're high-school girls, I
think, seniors in high school, probably, the kind of girls my
son will be dating any day now. One is . . . Zaftig is, I think,

the right word, she's heavier than the other one who is . . .
Voluptuous comes to mind. They are both dressed for the day, for
Halloween; they're dressed as fairies, I guess; they have wings
pinned to their backs and tiaras on their heads. The one girl is
very pretty as well as being voluptuous, and she has glitter
makeup on her face and on her . . . chest, parts of her glitter in
the early-afternoon light, and I move into the bus toward these
two girls, wondering if they might like to hear the story of my
accident, and they are smiling at me, and they both get up and
say, "Sir, would you like a seat?" On top of being zaftig and
voluptuous, they are polite young women. They had read the
sign on the back of their seats: "Won't you please give these
seats to the elderly and disabled?" And there I was! "Sit down!"
I snarled, and moved to the back of the bus.

(Music. PETER *picks up the comforter from the floor, wraps it around his
shoulders.)*

Actually, I could have used a seat . . .

(He picks up the yellow ball from the chair, and sits, holding the ball.)

I suddenly felt very tired.

*(*THE SHADOW *moves to behind the chair, leans down, crosses his arms over*
PETER'*s chest.* PETER *looks up, then reaches up and pulls the black hood
from* THE SHADOW'*s head, revealing him to be a red-haired boy of
fourteen.* GRIFF *kisses the top of* PETER'*s head, then lifts the yellow ball,
moves a short distance away.* PETER *looks at the bag.)*

I've got Death in this bag.

*(*GRIFF *turns to look at the bag. Something in the bag moves.* GRIFF *turns
away, lifts the yellow ball above his head. The yellow ball starts to glow.
The lights fade.)*

Proof

2000

> JEFF REICH

ORIGINAL PRODUCTION

DIRECTOR Kevin Confoy

SET DESIGNER Carlo Adinolfi

COSTUME DESIGNER Bruce Goodrich

SOUND Robert Gould

PROPS Laura Raynor

PRODUCTION STAGE MANAGER Jim Ring

STAGE MANAGER Christopher Lee

The cast was as follows:

NATHAN SIMPSON, PH.D. Brad Bellamy

PROFESSOR NORMAN P. CARVER Forest Compton

CHARACTERS

NATHAN SIMPSON, PH.D. forty-two-year-old British postdoctoral
fellow

PROFESSOR NORMAN P. CARVER seventy-nine-year-old American,
chairman of the Department of Neurobiology of a small upstate
university

PLACE

Upstate New York

TIME

Scene 1: The present
Scene 2: Later that night

SCENE 1

*A seminar room adjacent to the chairman's office in a small, red-brick, ivy-
covered university whose overall aged, dusty, broken-down look suggests a
once-proud institution in decline.*

*NATHAN stands by a lectern in the front of a lecture hall. Behind him
is an enormous floor-to-ceiling white screen upon which slides will be
projected. A blackboard is off to the right. He holds a cup of tea and a
stack of papers.*

NATHAN Welcome to the course on neuroscience. *(Pause.)* So much
for the introduction. Every year for the past five years I've given
this lecture. And every year for the past five years I am amazed
at how many of you manage to attend it. As the semester

proceeds you will see the wisdom in oversleeping. You will soon regard these lectures as a waste of valuable time. And your career in science as a waste of a valuable . . . well, anyway. There's a bunch of administrational-organizational-procedural and other things essential that I'm supposed to do, but I'm not going to. *(Pause. He puts the stack of papers aside.)* Lights. *(The lights dim.)* First slide, please.

(Slide #1 is upside down. It should read: "Neuroscience Seminar Topic #12: Nerve Regeneration," Nathan Simpson, Ph.D.")

Today's topic, slightly out of sequence if you're looking at your syllabus, is "Nerve Regeneration." In fact, it is supposed to be the very last lecture. Therefore, the information presented today will not make any sense. It will only confuse you, agitate you, and make you feel even more inadequate. A state of mind that will come to define your entire graduate experience. Nonetheless, it is a topic dear to the heart of your chairman, Professor Norman P. Carv . . . *(He notices the upside-down slide.)* Oh. Apparently this slide is upside down. It should say "Nerve Regeneration." That's the topic. The topic for today. And that's my name there, "Nathan Simpson"—postdoctoral fellow. Formerly, that is. Next slide, please.

(Slide #2 is also upside down. It is a black-and-white portrait of a gray-haired, stern-looking Norman Carver.)

It's not so much that I'm an expert, it's more that your chairman—Professor Norman Carver, who used to be but is no longer—can't be bothered. *(Noticing the slide is upside down.)* Oh. Apparently this slide is upside down, too. It's a picture of Professor Carver. Unfortunately, he couldn't be here on this your very first day of class. He's up at Lake Cayuga painting ferns. He sends his regards, by the way. You see, he asked me to fill in. He sent me a special message last night that said among other things: "Simpson, give your lecture to the new graduate students in the morning. And, oh, by the way, your funding has been canceled. You have no more grant. No more job. No more career. Essentially no future anymore in science." That was the message. That's how I found out. Essentially, that's how. Next slide, please.

(Slide #3 is once again upside down. It is a black-and-white picture of a goldfish.)

The study of nerve regeneration in the central nervous system takes advantage of the preserved ability of lower vertebrates—amphibian, reptile, fish—to regrow neuronal projections and reestablish synaptic connections. The model that we have used in Dr. Carver's lab is the . . . *(Notices the upside-down slide.)* . . . is the . . . umm . . . the goldfish retinal ganglion . . . ummm . . . *(Pause.)* Sorry. I guess I put this slide in upside down, too. It's a goldfish. An upside-down goldfish, as it were. A rather silly pet, if you ask me. Usually the object of murder by an otherwise innocent five-year-old with dirty hands. But to be honest, I don't think it's a really necessary slide. Everyone should know what a bloody goldfish looks like, for Chrissakes. Dr. Carver uses it mainly to fill up time. He shows pictures of fish and pictures of his painted ferns. It's really so transparent. Next slide, please.

(Slide #4—A black-and-white drawing of a fern.)

A fern. A painted fern. Next slide, please.

(Slide #5 is an upside-down schematic of a goldfish lesion experiment.)

A schematic. Finally a schematic. Ummm . . . an upside-down schematic, actually. Another upside-down slide, as it were. However, unlike the previous upside-down slides, this upside-down slide is a very necessary slide. Ummm . . . in fact, this one I absolutely should not have put in upside down. This one explains everything you need to know. It's really rather the critical one. Extremely important and totally uninterpretable like this. *(Pause.)* Sorry.

You see, loading slides correctly in one of those slotted slide carousel things has always been an impossible challenge for me. Like hitting a golf ball or playing three-dimensional chess or holding a baby. Especially without proper rest. You see, if I seem a little out of sorts this morning, it's because I didn't get much sleep last night. After I read Dr. Carver's message eight or nine times, I went for a long walk. I do that when I need to think. When I need to consider.

I made it all the way to the Happy Diner off Route 6. It looked like the right place. I ordered the Lumberjack Plate: three eggs, two links, a fried beefsteak, this round bacon-patty formulation, hash-brown potatoes, a buttered pancake, some buttered toast, buttered biscuits, a side dish of grits with nearly equal parts butter and a bottomless cup of coffee—$4.99. But the best part was asking the waitress to go at great inconvenience and fetch me some skimmed milk. Because after all, not only am I a strict vegetarian, but one with a strong family history of lipids and early heart disease. You could argue that this plate of Lumberjack food was otherwise an act of suicide. But if so, what a magnificent one. And at an incredible value, too. You see, I realized sitting there in the Happy Diner at 3 a.m. that vegetarians don't necessarily live longer, it just feels like you do. And why should I give a shit about pigs and cows and baby veals or the bloody farmer who kills them anymore, anyway. And I walked all the way back home and I smoked a pack of filterless cigarettes and I felt better than I have in years. Next slide, please.

(Slide #6 is a complicated graph of data from a goldfish lesion experiment.)
Back to goldfish. Nerve regeneration in goldfish, that is. You

might want to ignore this incomprehensible slide as well and listen. Put your pens down and just listen. You see, the beauty here is really rather simple. Majestic even. That is, if you lesion a goldfish's optic nerve—that is, dissect out the supraorbital cartilage and crush the optic nerve between the small ends of a jeweler's forceps—it will grow back. The optic nerve regenerates. *(Pause.)* I'll repeat that. The optic nerve regenerates. Do you understand how unbelievable that is? A mature, adult, fully formed goldfish swimming mindless in a bowl with one and only one reflexive thought—to eat shrimp flakes—yet it possesses the power to re-form an entire functional visual system. *(He waits, but there is no response.)* Nobody is impressed.

You see, I remember exactly where I was the first time I heard that: the Royal Academy of Science, October 14, 1975— the annual Sir Robert Boyle Oration. Now, instead of the usual Sir Robert Boyle Oration, there, rather at the front of the Royal Academy, was the indelible Norman Carver. He was the very first Yank to win the coveted Sir Robert Boyle Prize, and after that day perhaps the last. There, in classic Carver style, he presented what was, at the time, a pure brilliant discovery. A discovery that was, above all, as I thought sitting mesmerized, directed entirely at me. The idea seemed incredible. A goldfish regenerates an eye. A lowly, tasteless, and completely useless little anchovy could maintain the ultimate in self-determination: functional, immediate reincarnation. A goldfish could see again. And this fact, this simple footnote fact of nature, has since dominated my life. Next slide, please.

(Slide #7 is a blank slide. Projected on the screen is white light. As the surrounding lights dim, it is almost as if a spotlight forms on NATHAN.*)*

You see, I have a bachelor's degree in biology from a small college in Birmingham attended by working-class boys with no particular prepping, worthwhile fathers, or expected futures. And since there is no room for mediocrity on such a small island, as it were, I waved my mum "goodbye," shipped overseas, and landed like a modern-age Pilgrim on Plymouth Rock. Not exactly, more like Schenectady. Near Schenectady, actually, where I introduced myself to Professor Carver as a prospective doctorate in his lab for neurobiology. Now, twenty-one years and three months later, I am still in the middle of upstate nowhere, not doing much of anything except tending some Northeastern ferns, Xeroxing papers, and making sure the old bugger eats three fiber-heavy meals a day.

I have lived the proud migrant life of a science sharecropper. A mediocre Ph.D. who roams from grant to grant in search of the "truth," then a career, and finally a paycheck. And all during this martyrdom I have never even been considered for the Eucharist of a faculty position, let alone tasted drink from the holy grail of tenureship.

But please, please, please, I beg of you, please, don't pity me. Because I can assure you of this: neither will any of you. Because chances are a Ph.D. from an institution like this, a Ph.D. that will still take you five to six years of hard time to get, five to six years of indentured servitude, will amount to nothing. Nothing. So you can either sit there like gentle sheep unwittingly preparing for your own slaughter or you can rise up. Rise up with the fury of your youth and demand. *Demand* that your chairman, or your college dean, or the gods on Olympus provide you, if not a fighting chance, then at least a new vending machine for the lobby. I hear some can take dollar bills now and even cook chicken.

Now, I don't mean to be unduly harsh this early in the morning, but face facts: the chairman of your department is seventy-nine years old. He spent six years with Bob Finkel in the late forties doing voltage clamps and muscle physiology, and if you are unfortunate enough to wander past his office, he will sit you down and relive every painstaking detailed moment of it. He will explain how for thirty-five years he taught young men and women like you how to ask questions. How to find answers. How to get from A to Z over to and including P for proof. But somehow he will always manage to have one more paper, one more secret grant, one more promise, one more trick up his sleeve.

You see, if I have learned anything in a life of science, it is this: the world is finite. It occurred to me last night as I lay in bed staring at the ceiling for hours and hours and hours. I have traveled a great distance, spent twenty-one years and three months of my life in a lab, sacrificed thousands and thousands of little fish, and spent millions of your government's tax money to find out exactly four things. That's it. That's what my life has so far accomplished. Four things:

1. That a goldfish retinal ganglion cell regenerates.

2. That the whole thing takes exactly eighteen days in 20-degree water and fifteen days in 25-degree water.

3. That a 40-kilodalton glial protein seems to be important.

4. And that eyes or no eyes, the little buggers can still find the bloody shrimp flakes!

That's it. Four things. Four things that are of absolutely no use to anyone, least of all to goldfish. Four things that would not change the world in any way, shape, or form if these four things were not known. Or if I were not in it to know them.

So you wake up suddenly and you find you are no longer what you intended yourself to be. That you must face the most terrifying evidence of all.

Nature is supposed to abhor a vacuum. I have data. Some publications. Four facts added to the record. But after all these years of research and painstaking discovery, does one ever solve the most basic, most obvious, and most important question of them all? *(Pause.)* Are there no more slides?
(Blink to the next slide . . . Blackout.)

SCENE 2

Seminar room later. Lights up on PROFESSOR CARVER. *CARVER enters in his coat and with a briefcase. As the scene proceeds, he slowly takes off his coat and unpacks his bag while* NATHAN *is packing up his bags and putting on his coat.*

CARVER You dropped quite a bomb this morning, son. The students were shellshocked. Panicked. The dean deeply disturbed.

NATHAN I can explain that, sir.

CARVER Do you have any idea how humiliating it is to be stood up against the wall by a jittery crowd of fire-breathing students whose applications thirty years ago I wouldn't have used to line the inside of a cage? The nerve of them, son. Impeaching . . . crucifying me.

NATHAN I'm . . . I'm . . . I'm sure it'll blow over. I'm positive.

CARVER Prima donnas, if you ask me. Shouting about careers and publications, buttered eggs and vending machines. Did I ever tell you about when I was a doctoral student in Bob Finkel's lab?

NATHAN Many times, sir.

CARVER Finkel gave us a bench, a light source, and a . . .

NATHAN . . . kick in the ass.

CARVER Don't patronize me, boy.

NATHAN I've just heard that story, all the stories, before.

CARVER The bottom line is, nobody ever taught me anything. No one had to teach me anything. Did anyone teach you anything, son?

NATHAN No, sir. Nobody.

CARVER What do you mean "nobody"? What the hell have I been doing here all these years? Didn't I spend a career teaching young men like you things?

NATHAN Of course you have, sir, and we are all grateful.

CARVER Now don't get all sentimental either. Only thing I hate worse than ingratitude is false sentiment.

NATHAN I was being honest, sir.

CARVER I don't think you like me, Simpson.

NATHAN Since when do you care what anyone else thinks?

CARVER The truth is, I don't. Thirty-five years ago I built this department. For thirty-five years the mission of this department was to prepare young men like you how to ask questions, how to find . . .

NATHAN Proof, sir.

CARVER You blindsided me, you cowardly son-of-a-bitch. Hit-and-run. Assassination.

NATHAN All I told the students this morning was to look for the truth and beware. Be very aware.

CARVER Frankly, I didn't know you had that kind of fire in your belly, son. Didn't know you had the capacity to incite a riot like that. Didn't know.

NATHAN Frankly, neither did I.

CARVER Little more passion like that and you wouldn't be out of a job right now.

NATHAN I know deep down in your heart you mean that as a compliment. At least I want to believe that.

CARVER Believe what you want. Empiricism, Simpson. Remember.

NATHAN The fact is, I said what I felt. It was spontaneous. It was a sleepless night.

CARVER Look, I don't mind your being discouraged, but we're not going to take this lying down. We've got to fight.

NATHAN "Fight"?

CARVER Who is the head of that grant review committee? Stanley Schiff?

NATHAN Who?

CARVER Stanley Schiff and I go back forever. First-rate mouth, second-rate mind. Stanley said whatever he thought. No filter. Once an idea formed subfrontal, out it came.

NATHAN Professor Carver, we don't need any more funding.

CARVER We got a lab to run, boy.

NATHAN Not anymore.

CARVER The university grants are due any minute.

NATHAN The whats?

CARVER What do you think I've been counting on?

NATHAN A University Scholar's grant?

CARVER I think you're about ready for one of those.

NATHAN I've been long past ready for one of those.

CARVER That's exactly the point I'll make.

NATHAN Besides, I'm not eligible for a University Scholar's grant, sir. *(Pause.)* Why? Am I?

CARVER Now the boy's interested.

NATHAN I just don't think I'm still eligible, that's all.

CARVER 'Course you are. It's a three-year funded position. Fully sponsored.

NATHAN A chairman's letter is required for a Scholar's grant, sir.

CARVER What do you think I'm doing here?

NATHAN Why didn't you ever write one for me before?

CARVER You weren't ready before.

NATHAN And now I am? Now suddenly I am?

CARVER Quite possibly.

NATHAN Meaning?

CARVER Meaning, quite possibly.

NATHAN "Quite possibly" what?

CARVER You can't just get a University Scholar's grant like this.

NATHAN Like what?

CARVER Like this. With one foot out the door. How can I recommend you for anything like this?

NATHAN You're going to recommend me?

CARVER You and I, son, need to get back to work. Real work.

NATHAN Exactly what kind of "real" work, sir?

CARVER You've paid your dues. It'd be a shame to bail out right before you get your chance.

NATHAN You've known about those grants for years. Why did it never occur to you before, sir?

CARVER Why did it never occur to you, son? You've known about them, too. You could've easily applied yourself. But you didn't, did you? *(No response.)* Did you?

NATHAN No! I didn't. You know I didn't. I . . . I've always wanted to bring up the University Scholar's grants, sir, but I . . . well . . .

CARVER You're very quick to point fingers.

NATHAN I was just waiting for you to come to me, sir.

CARVER "Waiting"?

NATHAN I thought that if you considered my work worthy . . . well . . . then you would've initiated it. After all, you are the bloody chairman.

CARVER Someone to take care of you, is that it, son?

NATHAN Not exactly like that.

CARVER Suckle you?

NATHAN Please, sir!

CARVER What is it going to be, son?

NATHAN Are you being serious with me, sir? Completely serious? Are you?

CARVER Apparently the boy is going to question my commitment now, too, before the day is finally over.

NATHAN It's just that there's been so much, sir.

CARVER So much what? Bullshit? Listen up. Take what comes your way, boy. Best advice I ever got: "Take."

NATHAN It's not always so simple.

CARVER You think my life was so simple? So inevitable? I stumbled through it, son. Blindfolded. That's what we all do. Stumble. Did I ever tell you about the first time I met Bob Finkel?

NATHAN Hundreds of times, I'm afraid, sir.

CARVER The real truth is, I wandered into Finkel's lab by random chance.

NATHAN "By random chance"?

CARVER What do you think? I chose to be a biologist? I was twenty-one. What the hell did I know? The world was at war and I had little time to spare. I knocked on Finkel's door. He sat me down and went on to describe experiments in which he was able to take a simple impulse traveling down a nerve and freezeframe it. Voltage clamping, you see, and suddenly the fluid electricity that is the brain was within reach.

Now, I had not been raised religious, but at that moment I believed that if there was a God he had obviously retired on a full pension and ceded control of the universe to scientists like Bob Finkel.

Afterward Finkel just handed me a lab coat and a syllabus

and said two things. He said first, "From here on out you're a neuroscientist," and second, "Forget everything else."

NATHAN "Forget everything else"?

CARVER That's what he said.

NATHAN Apparently he was an even bigger son-of-a-bitch than you, sir.

CARVER Atta boy!

NATHAN Never thought it possible.

(They both laugh.)

CARVER You see, son, all I needed then and all I ever wanted was someone to believe in me.

NATHAN What does anyone ever need, sir?

CARVER I have a million stories like that, son. Wonderful stories like that. You see, that's why we have so much to do. My life, son. The story of my life.

NATHAN What about it, sir?

CARVER The grants. The University Scholar's grants.

NATHAN Yes, you said.

CARVER It's not just about me. It's about the modern age of neuro-science. The work, the people, the lives we lived. Men like Finkel, Sperry, Huxley. I mean, it was our time. And who better to tell it? Who better?

NATHAN I don't understand.

CARVER A memoir, son.

NATHAN A biography?

CARVER "Memoir" sounds more . . . more . . . I don't know . . . humble.

NATHAN That's what the Scholar's grant is for, sir?

CARVER Yes, for you . . . *(Pause.)* . . . and me.

NATHAN "You and me"?

CARVER We've got to be a team, son.

NATHAN A "team," sir?

CARVER Why are you repeating everything I say? Every damn thing? Listen to me. Listen to what I'm saying. *(He puts his arm on* NATHAN.*)* I believe in you, son. I do. *(Toasting)* Here's to you, my boy . . . cheers!

NATHAN You "believe" in me. Is that what you just said, sir? Now you believe in me? *(He takes a step back.)*

CARVER Look at you all of a sudden. Look at you looking at me like that.

NATHAN Until right now, never before in my lifetime of science did I ever have that singular moment of discovery. A moment when the true defining color of a man's light takes shape before my eyes.

CARVER Do you want consideration for a university grant or not?

NATHAN I see what you're trying to do, sir.

CARVER "Trying to do." I'm trying to run this department. For Chrissakes, we got work to do. Projects to design. Programs to run.

NATHAN I'm sorry, sir.

CARVER It's a new semester, Simpson. That means new students. Thesis planning. Hand-holding.

NATHAN Sir?

CARVER Let's get down to work, Simpson.

NATHAN *Sir?*

CARVER I'm trying to help you, son, aren't I?

NATHAN You are trying, but it's not for me. It's your web, sir. The web you so elegantly weave. I was never a match for you.

CARVER No, apparently not. First he lights the day on fire. Explodes in front of the students. Now ambushes me in here.

Yet the whole time he stands here. Stands here in a coat and his bags. Standing like some sort of monument, is that what you are, son?

NATHAN No monument, sir.

CARVER Like some sort of martyred tribute to himself. A legacy worthy of two little bags.

NATHAN You would rather I just turned and went, as if nothing? As if there was just nothing.

CARVER There is nothing. You've made sure of that.

NATHAN At the very least, sir. At the very least, maybe some kind of proper good-bye. A token, a letter, a pat on the back. Something that I finally, after all this time, don't bloody well have to ask for.

CARVER Oh, I see. Very well. *(He pats* NATHAN *on the back in mock tribute.)* Good-bye, Simpson. Close the door behind you. And leave your things. Regardless, that stuff belongs to the lab. It's a felony, you know. I'm well within my right, son.

NATHAN Stop calling me that! Please? Please. *(Pause.)* I'm not your . . . I never was.

CARVER Why are you trying to hurt me?

NATHAN You're afraid, too, aren't you, Professor Carver?

CARVER Afraid?

NATHAN You need me, you actually need someone, and that terrifies you.

CARVER You think it's so easy to walk away like this? I'll ruin your reputation before you get past the . . .

NATHAN Because maybe . . . maybe the terrifying truth is, I don't need anything from you anymore.

CARVER 'Course you don't. *(Pause.)* You . . . you . . . don't?

NATHAN You can't see yourself, can you? The great irony of my life so far is that you, whom I have always looked up to; you, who knows so much about how the nervous system works, really knows very little about how the nervous system works. I am very, very sorry, sir.

(CARVER *shuffles around somewhat lost.*)

CARVER How long have I known you, son?

NATHAN Forever, sir.

CARVER You're the only thing I have left. Do you realize that? The only thing.

NATHAN I don't think so, sir. A new semester started today. A class of new students for you. Pretty soon one will be at your side sending your telegrams, doing your lectures, tending your reveries. Don't worry, sir, you won't be alone.

CARVER Don't be so sure.

NATHAN Oh?

CARVER He took my chair away.

NATHAN Who took your chair away?

CARVER That dean. That little incubus of a man who occupies only a slight portion of the dean's chair. That's who.

NATHAN Why, what did he say?

CARVER He looked at me with his slicked-back ego and told me that I am no longer fit to be a chair in his college.

NATHAN Is that what he said?

CARVER Effective tomorrow. Ben Farley will be acting. I'm hereby professor emeritus. A university professor-at-large with an office somewhere in the basement. Out of the way, so I can't cause trouble. Out of the way to graze on dry leaves and hay. With my luck they'll put me next to that old quack Steinmetz from Physics. The one with the ponytail. Nothing I hate more than an eighty-five-year-old physicist with a ponytail.

NATHAN He took the whole lab away?

CARVER There might have been a chance with a university grant.

Perhaps. Funding, you know. *(Pause.)* I suppose I could stay up at the lake. I paint ferns. Local Northeastern ferns. Did I ever tell you that, son?

NATHAN Many times, sir.

CARVER A fern is simple, practical, poetic. Each leaf an exact replica. Fractals really. Structure subserving function. That's what science is about, my boy. Finding the structure, finding the meaning.

NATHAN Was this my fault, sir?

CARVER It's no one's fault. I ran out of ideas. You ran out of ideas. Can't do that in science nowadays. Things move fast. Way too fast. So what? Ideas are all around. Dance with them like I did. Or put them on a pedestal and admire. Sit back, relax, and admire. They're everywhere, son—everywhere.

NATHAN They were everywhere, sir. They were. But sometimes you don't have to look that far. *(He picks up his bags and turns to the door.)*

CARVER If you walk out that door, *Nathan* . . .

NATHAN You have lived a life, sir. A magnificent one. But it was yours.

CARVER It was a magnificent one, wasn't it? Spent six wondrous years with Bob Finkel. Whoever heard of neuroscience before us?

NATHAN No one, sir.

CARVER In 1975 I was the first American awarded the Sir Robert Boyle Prize.

NATHAN I know. I was there.

CARVER Now, I explained to your charming Queen that science awards are usually given to scientists at the end of their careers. But since I was a relatively young man and in complete control of a fully endowed chair and don't suffer the insular problem of vanity, perhaps there was someone else the Academy could find more worthy of the prize than me. Nonetheless, I humbly accept.

(He steps to the lectern. As the lights slowly dim around him, time moves back to October 14, 1975—the Sir Robert Boyle Oration.)

You see, I find nothing more exciting than the exchange of ideas. The pursuit of reason. Two words inscribed above the Oracle at Delphi. The two most important words in the history of mankind: "Know thyself." Imagine that: 2,545 years ago, men without microscopes, without silicon-chipped brains, without Sigmund Freud, for crying out loud, but still men who knew what made them men. "Know thyself." Science, you see. Next slide, please.

(The next slide is a bright gold-and-orange goldfish. NATHAN picks up his bag and exits.)

Ahhh . . . a goldfish . . .

(CARVER remains . . . fade out to black.)

Alien Boy

2000

>WILL SCHEFFER

ORIGINAL PRODUCTION

DIRECTOR Mark Roberts
SET DESIGNER Carlo Adinolfi
COSTUME DESIGNER Bruce Goodrich
SOUND Robert Gould
PROPS Laura Raynor
PRODUCTION STAGE MANAGER Jim Ring

The cast was as follows:
ALIEN BOY David Greenspan

CHARACTERS

ALIEN BOY

PLACE

Bloomfield, New Jersey

Howard Johnson's. Sousa march blares as the lights fade. Lights up.

ALIEN BOY Today I am thirteen.
(Sound: a nuclear bomb exploding.)

I don't want to be thirteen. I have always yearned to be older than my years. Therefore I have been described as a precocious child. I drink coffee. I smoke cigarettes. I use the words masturbatory, ennui, and existential liberally in conversation. But today I am thirteen. I am wearing my sailor suit. I come down here often in my sailor suit, to the Howard Johnson's in Bloomfield, New Jersey, and I wait. I wait for a man to come and take me away, away from this childhood that I do not belong in. A blond man who is muscular and bold, I have seen him on TV. He will teach me how to be athletic and brave. He will give structure and meaning to my life. He will hold me in the dark. Just we two. I wait and wait. But he never seems to come.

(He lights a cigarette.)

I was supposed to be bar mitzvahed today. But I told my mother I wouldn't go. I told her that I decided I didn't want to be Jewish anymore. My mother was distraught. "You can't just decide you don't want to be Jewish anymore," she said. I told her again: "I don't want to be Jewish." "Why don't you want to be Jewish?" she asked me. "In the street, children throw pennies at me, they call me Jew Bagel. In an age when it is possible for us to choose our own destiny, I have decided I don't want to go through life with the particular disadvantage of being a Jew. I want to be blond and handsome like the men on TV. I want to drive a Volkswagen." "Over my dead body you'll drive a Volkswagen. This wouldn't be happening if your father were alive." "He's not alive," I said, "he's dead!" My mother took a Valium and locked herself in her bedroom.

(Sound: a door slamming.)

My father was a Jew.

(He lights another cigarette.)

He came to America during World War II. He was—an alien.

(Music: "Psycho.")

He left behind his mother, his sister, his first wife, and a son. They died at Auschwitz. I have their names here, as listed by the Red Cross. Rebecca, Betsy, Rachel, and the son, Wolf, who was shoveled into an oven on the day of his thirteenth birthday in 1943.

(Sound: fire. Combustion. He burns the names of his relatives with flash paper.)

I never got along with my father. He spoke with a heavy foreign accent. He was thin and pale and European, not at all like the men on TV. One day I was walking around the house in my mother's high heels and my father caught me. He slapped me and told me: "I never want you to walk in high heels again. Soon you will be thirteen, you will be bar mitzvahed; soon you will be a man." "I don't want to be a man," I told him. "*You're* a man, I wish you were dead." The next year he died of lung cancer. Now I wear my mother's high heels whenever she's not at home.

(He puts on high heels. "I Feel Pretty" from West Side Story *plays as* ALIEN BOY *twirls.)*

I turn up the music from *West Side Story* and I twirl my baton. *(When the lyrics reach: "I feel pretty, and witty, and gay" . . . the music stops with a screech and horror music fades in.)*

Last night after my mother had cooked me a Swanson frozen TV dinner, I was reading *Everything You Wanted to Know About Sex But Were Afraid to Ask* by David Reuben, M.D., and I quote:

(Voice-over)

"Male homosexuality is a condition in which men have a driving emotional and sexual interest in other men. Because of the anatomical and physiological limitations involved, there are some formidable obstacles to overcome. In the process they often transform themselves into part-time women. They don women's clothes, wear makeup, adopt feminine mannerisms, and occasionally even try to rearrange their bodies along feminine lines."

I don't want to be a homosexual. Until last night I didn't know I was one. I knew I was different, but I didn't think there was a name for it. I knew I liked to wear my mother's slip. I knew I liked to wrestle with my friend Nicky Sabatini, and I knew I didn't mind losing. I knew I liked to rub against the sofa watching Monty Hall on *Let's Make a Deal*, and the cowboys on *Bonanza*. But then I read this:

(Voice-over)

"Some of the more routine items that find their way into the gastrointestinal systems of homosexuals via the exit are pens, pencils, lipsticks, combs, pop bottles, ladies' electric shavers, and enough other items to stock a small department store."

(Sound: electric shaver.)

I definitely don't want to be a homosexual. One day, after we finish wrestling, Nicky Sabatini tells me that there is a movie called *Boys in the Band*, about homos. I decide that I must see this movie, that perhaps it will shed light on this condition, this horrible thing that is me. I ask my mother to take me. I need her to take me because children are not permitted to see it unless accompanied by their legal guardian. "What's it about?" she asks. "About a group of musicians." "Why do you want to see it so bad?" "Because, as you know, I am learning how to play the tuba, and my motivation is already failing because it's so hard to carry it back and forth to school." My mother agrees to take me, because she will do anything to encourage my musicality. We go to the Royal Theater that night for the eight o'clock show.

(Sousa music.)

When we get to the theater, the woman who sells tickets will not let me in. She says the movie is unsuitable for children my age. I demand to see the manager. "It's illegal," I say, "what you're doing." The lady calls the manager. He is from a foreign country. He can't believe my mother would take me to see such a movie. "Do you know what it's about?" he asks her. "Musicians," she answers. He pulls her away from me and talks to her in hushed foreign tones. When she returns she tells me we can't enter. "I'm sorry, why don't we go to the Welmont Theater to see *Snow White and the Seven Dwarfs*? I start to throw a fit. "It's illegal, what they're doing," I say again. "I'm going to write a letter." My mother takes me across the street to Woolworth's and offers to buy me a Hot Wheels set. "I don't want it," I say. I hold out until she buys me a G.I. Joe doll. She takes me home and makes me Jell-O.

The next evening I convince my mother that it is her civic responsibility to allow me to see *Boys in the Band*. "This is

America," I remind her. "It's a free country." Finally, she agrees to take me to a theater in New York City, where we have no trouble gaining admittance.

(*The lights dim, music: "Heatwave."*)

As we sit in the darkness, I nervously eat a pack of Goobers and Raisinets. My mother fidgets and allows a pack of Eskimo Pies to melt uneaten onto her ecru pants suit. We watch together in horror as a group of genuine homosexuals complain about their mothers and dance together in a conga line—and as we watch, a subtle electricity flows back and forth between my mother and myself, an unmistakable unspoken acknowledgment that now we both understand why I wanted to see this movie. When we leave the theater we are silent, in tacit agreement that we will not mention the horrible truth that somewhere deep inside us, we have both, in this moment, come to know.

(*Sci-fi music plays. Lights flash outside the window.*)

That night I have a disturbing dream. Outside my window I see strange lights. A spaceship lands and a robot man descends from its steps and comes into my bedroom. He is very blond and looks like my G.I. Joe doll and the devastatingly handsome Nazis I have seen in war films. He comes to my bed and takes me on his lap. He looks very cold, like metal, but when he touches me, his skin is hot. He holds me in his hot arms. He says: "You must tell me that you love me." I look into his blond eyes. I start to form the words "I love you." "I . . . love . . ." I wake up screaming.

(*Sound: a horror-movie scream.*)

It's two in the morning. In *Boys in the Band* all the homosexuals had psychiatrists. I creep into the kitchen and go for the Yellow Pages. I look under the letter P. I find the names of all the psychiatrists in Bloomfield. Both of them. Dr. Kaplan and Dr. Casey. I choose Dr. Casey, because he sounds more attractive. I write him a brief letter: "Dear Dr. Casey: I think I am a homosexual. I have no money. I cannot tell my mother. Please help me. I want to be cured." I find a stamp in my mother's pocketbook. For the rest of the night I dream of my doctor. The one who will save me. The man I've been waiting for.

The next day, while carrying my tuba, I mail the letter to my doctor. The boys at school have stopped calling me Jewboy and have begun to call me pussy and faggot. I now dress in work boots and flannel shirts to disguise myself. Anxious weeks pass as daily I run home after school to check the mailbox. Every night I stay awake until four, praying to the God I do not believe in to save me from my sordid fate. Then one day a letter arrives addressed to me.

(Vicki Carr singing: "Dear God It Must Be Him." The ALIEN BOY *clutches the letter to his chest and opens it, his heart pounding.)*

He will see me one week from today in his office. I am filled with excruciating anticipation. The week passes quickly, and on the day of our assignation I run from school to the bus that will take me to my hero. I have dressed in my argyle shirt and socks, corduroy bell-bottoms and platform shoes, tempting derogatory slurs from the boys in gym class, but I don't care, I am reckless with expectation.

I arrive at Dr. Casey's office. I ring the bell and am buzzed into a small waiting room. "I'm here to see Dr. Casey," I say to the secretary with a hint of pride. As she knocks suspiciously on the doctor's door I look around his office. I am disappointed to find other people here. The secretary returns and ushers me into Dr. Casey's office. Suddenly, as I am face-to-face with the man who knows my secret, I realize why I have felt vaguely disoriented since arriving. Dr. Casey is a black person, like his secretary and the people in the waiting room. I am momentarily unable to process this information, as I have never seen a black doctor on TV. But the look of kindness on his handsome face reassures me. I imagine my small white face pressed against his strong black chest. The secretary leaves and the doctor asks me a few questions. "Why do you think you are a homosexual?" "Because I like men," I tell him. "What do you want to do with them?" "I don't know—just be with them," I offer, searching for the correct answers, "and give them blow jobs." "Where did you learn that word?" "In *Everything You Always Wanted to Know About Sex* by David Reuben, M.D.," I reply. Dr. Casey seems satisfied with my answers and then rises from behind his desk. "I'd like to help you," he says, "but you understand, I can't possibly treat you without the permission of your mother."

(Horror music.)

He hands me the phone. "I'm afraid you'll have to call her and tell her where you are."

(Sound: air-raid sirens.)

I dial my mother's phone number at work, unable to look him in the eyes. "Hello, Mom?" "I'm at a doctor's office." "No, nothing's wrong."

I hand the phone to Dr. Casey. "I think you should come down and pick your son up," he says. "313 Franklin Street." He hangs up the phone. "I'm sorry," he says. I look into Dr. Casey's eyes. *(Pause.)* "I . . . you . . . nigger!"

(Sound: a horror-movie scream. The ALIEN BOY *puts his hands over his ears. Beat.)*

My mother collects me at Dr. Casey's office, and she tells him: "What he's lacking is a male role model." Dr. Casey agrees and offers to treat me, but my mother nervously replies, "There is a Dr. Kaplan in town, who I think would be a more appropriate choice for us." We walk briskly to the car. We sit in front of Dr. Casey's office in silence. My mother lights a cigarette.

"Why didn't you tell me about this . . . problem?" "There is no problem, I feel better already." "Really, I think it's just a passing phase you're going through." "Yes, I feel it passing already as we speak." "What would you like for dinner?" "Can we go to McDonald's?" "Yes, I think that's a wonderful idea."

And that's the last we talk about it. Years pass.

I look at myself in the mirror as I prepare to meet my mother in New Jersey. After thirty years I must admit my boyish good looks and full head of hair have not diminished. I look remarkably like my dead father. An irony I am not unaware of.

I take the bus from New York City to my mother's small apartment. We see each other often, my mother and me. We share an easy intimacy. As easy as either of us is capable of. We even talk about my boyfriends.

Tonight my mother's taking me to dinner at McDonald's. Close and within walking distance, it is most convenient now that she doesn't drive anymore.

(Muzak.)

I haven't been to a McDonald's in years, but it's the same as I remember it. It's different, but it hasn't really changed. It's like Cher.

My mother and I eat Big Macs and talk about current events. My mother is ecstatic about the passing of the Gay Marriage Bill in Vermont. She looks forward to the day I settle down with someone. She wants me to have the kind of love she had with my father. To not be lonely.

"Are you lonely?" I ask her. "No, no. I have so many friends," she says. "Why didn't you ever remarry?" "After your father, there was nobody else for me. You know that." "Do you miss him?" she asks. "Yes," I answer. "I miss him very much."

She delicately chews on a french fry. "I miss him, too." She takes a gulp of diet Sprite. McDonald's seems to be making her nostalgic.

"But I wish I had done a better job with you . . . after . . . ," she says. "You know, I still feel bad about when you went to see that psychiatrist—what was his name?" "Dr. Casey," I answer. "I should never have made him call me." "Oh, Ma," I say, "you're confused. He made ME call YOU. He was a bad psychiatrist. He betrayed my trust."

And then it all comes out.

"No. I never told you this, but I opened that letter you got from Dr. Casey, you know, saying he would see you. I made him have you call me from his office.

"I told him I'd sue him if he didn't. I was so desperate to know why you contacted him. I didn't know what else to do."

(Sound: sirens.)

And suddenly it feels as if I am falling. As if the room around me is falling away.

"Darling." "I'm sorry." "Please forgive me." "I love you."

"It's okay," I say. I stare at my hot apple pie. "You did the best you could." I start to form the words "I love you." "I . . . love . . ." Inside myself I hear the roar of wind and the sound of combustion.

"I love you, Ma. I forgive you. I love you. Of course, I love you."

(Music: "Heatwave" bumps up.)

And suddenly the flames of love engulf me. I see the plastic chairs begin to melt. The tables are bursting into fire. I smell the stench of burning flesh, and as McDonald's is consumed, I scream for help . . .

Then all at once my dead father appears and takes my hand. He pulls my mother to her feet. With him are *his* mother, Rebecca, his sister Rachel, his first wife, Betsy, and their son, Wolf. Dr. Casey joins us—and David Reuben, M.D. . . . As the plastic burns around us, we all begin to dance together.

We form a huge conga line and we dance. We dance and we dance and we dance, through the flames.

(Lights fade.)

The Rothko Room

2000

> STUART SPENCER

ORIGINAL PRODUCTION

DIRECTOR John Ruocco
SET DESIGNER Chris Jones
COSTUME DESIGNER Julie Doyle
SOUND Robert Gould
PROPS Laura Raynor
PRODUCTION STAGE MANAGER Jim Ring
STAGE MANAGER Jason Carroll

The cast was as follows:
DENNIS Dashiell Eaves
ALICE Christine Farrell

CHARACTERS

DENNIS
ALICE

PLACE

The Tate Gallery, London

TIME

The present

The Rothko room. A low bench in the middle of the room. We see a suggestion of large canvases by Rothko—the Seagram murals.

    ALICE *sits on the bench. Her shoes are off, lying in front of her. She is looking at a particular painting on the fourth wall.*

    DENNIS *stands to one side, studying a different painting. He doesn't seem to see her—she is always just out of his peripheral vision. He comes around to the same painting she is looking at, stands very close to it, and studies it. It becomes obvious that he is blocking her view of it. She sighs. Clears her throat. The sound alerts* DENNIS, *who turns around to see the problem.*

DENNIS Oh! Sorry . . .
ALICE It's all right . . .
DENNIS Didn't see you there . . .
ALICE It's quite all right . . .
(DENNIS *stands aside. They both look at the paintings. After a moment, he glances her way. She is looking at the painting. He looks back at it also. A pause for thought . . .*)

DENNIS They're all portals.

ALICE Excuse me?

DENNIS That simple blank wash. Then the outline, like a door. Like a window. Archway. Stage curtain. Over and over. That's what gives the room cohesion. They're each a form of entrance, a gateway into . . . something.

ALICE *(Letting it register, but not entirely sure yet)* Yes . . .

DENNIS Obvious, when you think about it.

ALICE Obvious but . . . subtle.

DENNIS Well, you wouldn't want *Doorway* written under every one.

ALICE I should say not.

DENNIS Do you have a favorite?

ALICE Uh . . . well . . . those two, I think—down at the end.

(DENNIS turns to look. We can see them also.)

DENNIS *(Disappointed)* Oh.

ALICE What?

DENNIS Those two—they're the only ones that are . . .

ALICE Yes?

DENNIS . . . not portals.

ALICE Oh.

DENNIS They're ground plans.

ALICE *(Looking at them)* How can you tell?

DENNIS Well, you see—you're not looking *through* something. You're looking *down*. From above. Bird's-eye view. Like the site of an excavation. That's the outline of the building there. See?

ALICE *(Dawning . . .)* Oh . . . yes. All right.

DENNIS *(Leaving these behind)* But the rest of them, these—they're all portals to another place.

ALICE *(Taking them in)* Yes. Well, I can certainly see that. Yes.

(DENNIS sits down next to her.)

DENNIS *(Modestly)* Standard interpretation.

ALICE Really.

DENNIS Oh, sure.

ALICE I never would have thought of it—

DENNIS I read it in a book.

ALICE Very informative. Thank you.

DENNIS Your first time?

ALICE Yes. I just happened to be walking in the neighborhood and I thought, Why not? *(She looks at the paintings again.)* But that was quite helpful. Thank you.

DENNIS The question is, what place? Portals to where?

ALICE *(Surprised; she looks back at the paintings again.)* I don't know.

DENNIS One doesn't know, does one.

ALICE No . . .

DENNIS Almost as if he didn't *want* us to know.

ALICE *(Still looking at them)* No . . .

DENNIS As if he wanted it a secret.

ALICE *(Confirmed now)* Yes.

DENNIS Not to know.

ALICE Not literally, anyway.

DENNIS Right, exactly.

ALICE Where do you think they go?

(DENNIS looks at her as if surprised by the question, as if seeing her now for the first time. He almost studies her.)

DENNIS Where have you been?

ALICE Well, I . . . What do you mean?

DENNIS You happened to be in the neighborhood. Where were you going?

ALICE Nowhere special.

DENNIS No particular destination?

ALICE Well . . . here, I suppose. This *became* my destination. I realized it as I walked in. Doesn't that ever happen to you? You arrive, then you think, Yes, this is it.

DENNIS Interesting.

ALICE Is it?

DENNIS Well, you know the story of how *they* . . . *(Gestures toward the paintings.)* . . . got here.

ALICE No.

DENNIS They were meant as a mural for some restaurant. A famous one, I forget the name, but very famous. In New York City. A commission. But he finishes them and he thinks, I don't want my paintings looking down on some rich bastards chewing their bloody sirloins. So he returns the commission and he keeps the paintings. For ten years they sit. Nothing. Then *this* place offers to buy them, and he says, "All right, but on one condition: they get their own room, with the lighting just so—like this, very dark, and they all stay together. *It* stays together, the mural, forever."

ALICE And not a sirloin steak in sight.

DENNIS So the gallery says, All right. That's fine. We accept your condition. The paintings arrive and on that morning they get a call from overseas, from the dealer in New York. That night, while the paintings were high up over the Atlantic, on their way here—at that very moment, he killed himself. *(He looks at the paintings. Alice looks at them, too, as if for the first time.)* See what I mean?

ALICE I'm not sure.

DENNIS It was *his* destination also.

ALICE Like a letter from a dead man.

(DENNIS looks at her for a moment . . .)

DENNIS How could you leave like that?

ALICE Dennis, don't.

DENNIS No? Why shouldn't I?

ALICE This was going so well.

DENNIS Why did you leave?

ALICE I didn't *leave.*

DENNIS Oh really?

ALICE Well, I'm here, aren't I? I'm here now. *(DENNIS looks at her angrily. Then he looks at the painting on the fourth wall for a long moment, silent. She looks at it, too. A pause.)* If you look long enough, they start to shimmer.

DENNIS Yes?

ALICE Vibrate, almost. This one in particular. *(She nods at the fourth wall. Dennis looks at her skeptically.)* Go ahead, look. *(He looks. A long pause.)* Do you see?

DENNIS No.

(ALICE's eyes don't leave the canvas.)

ALICE Go stand right up next to it.

DENNIS What do you mean?

ALICE Eighteen inches is the perfect distance. *(DENNIS looks at her skeptically.)* That's what *he* says. *(A nod at the painting, indicating she means Rothko.)*

DENNIS How do you know?

ALICE It's in the flyer. *(She indicates the museum brochure.)* Go ahead. Go right up to it. *(DENNIS stands and walks far downstage, facing the audience. He is inches from the painting.)* Give it a moment. *(DENNIS continues to look. Another long pause.)* Yes?

DENNIS *(After a moment, still looking. There's a glimmer, but he's still not sure.)* Mmmm.

ALICE Yes?

DENNIS *(Suddenly, as if he's had a revelation)* Yes.

ALICE As if there's something behind . . . something *else.*

ENSEMBLE STUDIO THEATRE MARATHON 2000

DENNIS *(Still looking, caught up in the experience)* When did you notice this?

ALICE I just—I don't know. I found myself watching it and it started to shimmer—

DENNIS Yes.

ALICE Tremble almost. And there's nothing but the painting.

DENNIS Nothing, no . . .

ALICE Shimmering, vibrating . . .

DENNIS Lambent.

ALICE Beautiful, but . . .

(Slight pause.)

DENNIS *(Still looking)* But what?

ALICE But . . . not beautiful.

DENNIS Yes. Beautiful. And . . . *not* beautiful. That's exactly it. *(He steps away from the painting, turning to look at her, though he stays where he is. She starts to put on her shoes.)*

DENNIS You can't go *now*.

ALICE That's all I wanted to do. I wanted you to see that.

DENNIS Wanted me to see what?

ALICE *(Not really paying attention; struggling to get her shoe on.)* That it shimmers. That there's something *there*.

DENNIS Yes, and what else?

ALICE What do you mean, what else? What else is there?

DENNIS But why does it shimmer?

ALICE I can't explain that.

DENNIS Then why are you telling me?

ALICE I'm not telling you. I asked you to look, and you did. You looked, you *saw*.

DENNIS There's got to be more to it than that. You must know *why*.

ALICE It shimmers because that's what it does.

DENNIS And why should it do that?

ALICE I told you, I can't explain.

DENNIS Because something is on the other side? Because we can see through to the other side?

ALICE Yes, I've told you.

DENNIS Then what is it? What's on the other side?

ALICE If I could tell you, I would. But there's nothing I could say that would explain. If I could, there wouldn't be any reason for the painting. *(Her shoe is on. She starts to go.)*

DENNIS This is worse than the fact that you left in the first place. Do you know that? Or is it that you just don't care?

(This cuts. ALICE *turns impatiently. She looks at the fourth-wall painting, then at* DENNIS.*)*

ALICE All right, what do *you* see?

DENNIS I just told you.

ALICE Behind that. The reason for all that shimmering.

DENNIS *(Slight pause. Considering)* I don't want to say.

ALICE Why not?

DENNIS I don't want to think it.

ALICE Why not?

DENNIS Because it's . . . it's not . . . It's like you said: It's something . . . not beautiful.

ALICE And?

*(*DENNIS *looks again.)*

DENNIS It's like the flickering of a candle.

ALICE So?

DENNIS Like a flame.

ALICE And?

DENNIS And it scares me.

ALICE It can be frightening, yes.

DENNIS *(Sarcastically)* Well, that's very comforting. Thanks a lot.

(DENNIS *turns away.* ALICE *takes a moment to reconsider.*)

ALICE Sunlight.

DENNIS *(Confused)* What? I'm sorry, but I don't . . .

ALICE That's the closest way to say it. Sunlight. It's a flame, after all, isn't it? A terrible, blinding burning. But at the same time, quite beautiful. The most beautiful thing there is.

DENNIS *(Realization)* That's true.

ALICE Isn't it.

DENNIS You're right.

ALICE So, in a sense . . .

DENNIS Yes.

(Beat. ALICE *goes back to the other subject.*)

ALICE It had nothing to do with you.

DENNIS No, I know that.

ALICE Do you? Really?

DENNIS Well, it sometimes *feels* as though . . . maybe . . . I wasn't—Oh, this is stupid . . .

ALICE What?

DENNIS Worthy.

ALICE Well, that's all it was. A feeling. If you think about it, if you really try to *understand*—you'll know it was just . . . I had to go. There wasn't any choice. Yours, mine, anyone's. It was time for me to go. Everyone has their time. I've had mine, you'll have yours.

DENNIS I was so *angry.* I'm still angry—even now . . .

ALICE Of course. Who wouldn't be?

DENNIS Really? You think?

ALICE *(Laughing)* Oh, *please.* Furious!

DENNIS I kept—I just assumed I was somehow . . . I don't know. A crank of some kind.

ALICE You're not a crank. Well, you are—talking to yourself in galleries, after all.

DENNIS Don't say that.

ALICE What?

DENNIS "Talking to myself . . ." You're here. I know you are.

ALICE Yes, but imagine what someone would see if they walked in right now.

(Slight pause.)

DENNIS You know, I wonder.

ALICE Wonder what?

DENNIS If I knew that you would be here. Not *knew*, but somehow *felt* . . .

ALICE You were ready to see me. That's all.

DENNIS But why now? I've missed you so long.

ALICE Today you were ready. I don't know why. One never knows why. Even *he* doesn't try to tell us why. *(A nod to the painting again, indicating Rothko.)*

DENNIS Do you really have to go?

ALICE I think I ought to, now.

DENNIS Hold my hand, would you? *(Alice takes his hand. He presses it with his other hand.)* Thank you for . . .

ALICE Making this my destination?

DENNIS Yes . . . that's it, isn't it. You were . . . bidden. And you came.

(ALICE smiles indulgently.)

ALICE If you'd like another minute, you could walk out with me.

DENNIS No.

ALICE Then you're staying.

DENNIS I can't walk out with you. I'd only have to say good-bye to you someplace else. Better it were here.

ALICE That's very smart. You were always such a smart boy. I worried about my other children when I had to go. But I never worried about you. You were so young, the youngest. But even then I knew how smart you were. And I knew you'd be fine.

DENNIS Good-bye. *(He presses her hand one more time, then turns to study another painting.)*

ALICE I think you're wrong about those two, though. I think they're also doors. I think they're all doors.

(ALICE stays for just a moment, then realizes it's time for her to go—the signal has already been given. She turns silently and exits. DENNIS watches her go. Then he sits and studies the painting as the lights fade.)

Notes on Contributors

BILLY ARONSON's plays have been published in *The Best American Short Plays of 1992–1993* and *Plays from Woolly Mammoth Theatre*. He has been awarded a NYFA grant, and his plays are often performed at EST. His writing for the musical theater includes the original concept and additional lyrics for *Rent* and librettos for operas commissioned by American Opera Projects with music by Rusty Magee and Kitty Brazelton. His TV writing includes scripts for Children's Television Workshop, MTV, and the Cartoon Network.

LESLIE AYVAZIAN is the author of *Nine Armenians*, which has been performed around the country and has won numerous awards, including the John Gassner Outer Critics Circle Award for best new play and the Susan Smith Blackburn International Play Award; *Singer's Boy*, which premiered at the Geary Theatre in San Francisco; *Practice*; and several one-acts produced at EST, including *Deaf Day*, which appeared in the *Ensemble Studio Theatre Marathon '99* anthology (Faber, 2000). Her latest work, *High Dive*, a one-person performance piece, premiered at the Long Wharf Theatre in November 2000. Ayvazian has taught playwriting at Columbia University, Sarah Lawrence College, and Drew University, as well as at Playwrights Horizons and EST.

EDWARD ALLAN BAKER has written ten one-act plays for the EST Marathon. He is the author of numerous plays produced off-Broadway, including *Prairie Avenue*. He has also written for Showtime and HBO. His one-act play *Dolores* was published in *The Best American Short Plays of 1989*. He is a member of the Sarah Lawrence theater faculty.

LESLIE CAPUTO is a writer for both stage and screen. She co-authored the award-winning nonfiction book *Teenage Fathers* with Karen Gravelle, Ph.D. Other one-act plays include *Fade to White*, *Dodging Charlie*, *Mullberry Street Beauties*, *Daryl's 21st*, and *Vacation from Hester and Allen*. She has written two full-length plays, *Bleecker Street Comics* and *The Actor's Home*, and a trilogy of one-acts, of which *Birth Marks* is the first act. She is a member of the Ensemble Studio Theatre and the Actors Studio Process Unit for Playwrights.

HEATHER DUNDAS is the author of *Ghost Stories*, a collection of short plays which includes *Cannibals*; three full-length plays: *Memory Game*, *Rules for Cheaters*, and *Body Count*; and several short plays for children. Among her upcoming projects is a ten-minute history of human evolution as told through gossip and rumors, which was commissioned by the Virginia Avenue Project, the West Coast branch of New York's 52 Street Project. She is a member of Circle Rising and the Echo Theater Company.

STEVE FEFFER's plays have been produced or developed by theaters that include EST, the O'Neill National Playwrights Conference, Philadelphia Festival Theatre for New Plays, the National Jewish Theatre in Chicago, Playwrights Theatre of New Jersey, and Stages Repertory Theatre in Houston. His play *The Wizards of Quiz* was published by Dramatists Play Service, and a number of his short theater pieces were published by Heinemann Books. Steve Feffer has a BFA in Dramatic Writing from New York University, an MFA from the University of Iowa's Playwrights Workshop, and is currently in the Ph.D. program in Theater and Drama at the University of Wisconsin, Madison.

DAVID IVES was born in Chicago and educated at Northwestern University and the Yale School of Drama. A Guggenheim Fellow in playwriting, he is best known for his evening of one-act comedies called *All in the Timing*. The show won the Outer Critics Circle Playwriting Award, ran for two years off-Broadway, and, in the 1995–96 season was, after Shakespeare productions, the most performed play in the country. He is also the author of one other evening of short comedy, *Mere Mortals*, and a children's novel, *Monsieur Eek*. Among his full-length plays are *Ancient History*, *Don Juan in Chicago*, and *The Red Address*.

WARREN LEIGHT is the author of *Side Man*, which was produced on Broadway, won the 1999 Tony Award for Best Play, and was nominated for a Pulitzer Prize. His plays produced off-Broadway include *Stray Cats*; the musical *Mayor*, a Drama Desk nominee for best book; *Loop*, also known as *Five Bedrooms*; and *High-Heeled*

Women, which won the Outer Critics Circle Award. His latest play, *Glimmer, Glimmer and Shine*, was produced at the Mark Taper Forum in January 2001. He is also the author of *Big Street*, an upcoming Damon Runyan musical, along with Alan Menken and Marion Adler. His writing for the screen includes *The Night We Never Met*, which he also directed; *Me and Him*; and *Before the Nickelodeon*.

ROMULUS LINNEY is the critically acclaimed author of three novels and over thirty plays staged throughout the United States and abroad, including *The Sorrows of Frederick*, *Holy Ghosts*, and *Tennessee*. His stories have appeared in many literary journals, there are four volumes of his plays, and his one-acts have been included in numerous short-play anthologies. He has received two Obies, one for Sustained Excellence in Playwriting, and both the Award in Literature and the Award of Merit Medal from the American Academy of Arts and Letters. His work is frequently produced at EST.

PETER MALONEY is an actor, director, and writer. His plays *Lost and Found*, *Pastoral*, and *Last Chance Texaco* were published by Samuel French, Inc. After premiere productions at the Ensemble Studio Theatre, they have been produced at theaters across America. A recent play, *In the Devil's Bathtub*, was published in *The Kenyon Review*. His adaptation of Machiavelli's *Mandragola* was commissioned by the Folger Shakespeare Theatre and opened there under his direction. He is an alumnus of the New Dramatists and a member of EST and the Actors Studio. He is the recipient of a Fox Foundation Fellowship for the year 2000.

JEFF REICH's *Proof* was originally commissioned by the Ensemble Studio Theatre/ Alfred J. Sloan Foundation Science and Technology Project, 1999. His full-length *The Milgram Experiments* was awarded an EST/Alfred J. Sloan Foundation Science and Technology Project commission for 2000. Other plays include *Chrissy*, *DNR*, *Joe and Sarah*, *Ersatz Nevada*, *Sonny Boy*, and *Train*.

WILL SCHEFFER is a playwright and screenwriter. His play *Easter* was made into a feature film in 2000. *Alien Boy* is his fourth play to be produced in the EST Marathon. Scheffer received a Cable Ace Award, a Christopher Award, and a Writers Guild Award for his adaptation of Alice Elliott Dark's short story *In the Gloaming* for HBO.

STUART SPENCER's play *Resident Alien* received numerous productions around the country in the 2000 season and is in development as a motion picture. His other plays include *In the Western Garden*, which was published in the *Ensemble Studio Theatre Marathon '99* anthology (Faber, 2000); *Blue Stars*, which was selected for *The Best American Short Plays of 1993–1994*; *Suddenly Devotion*; and *Go to Ground*. A three-play anthology, *Plays by Stuart Spencer*, was recently published by Broadway Play Publishing, and his playwriting primer, *The Playwright's Guidebook*, will be published by Faber and Faber in 2001. He is working on a new play commissioned by South Coast Rep. Spencer teaches playwriting in private classes and at Sarah Lawrence College. He is a member of EST and the Dramatists Guild.

Permissions